# WE ARE AMUSED
## A ROYAL MISCELLANY

# WE ARE AMUSED

## A ROYAL MISCELLANY

*Everything you wanted to know
about the Royal Family...
but didn't know who to ask*

## BRIAN HOEY

First published in Great Britain in 2010 by
JR Books, 10 Greenland Street, London NW1 0ND
www.jrbooks.com

A catalogue record for this book is available from the British Library.

ISBN 978-1-906779-85-6

1 3 5 7 9 10 8 6 4 2

Printed by Clays Ltd, St Ives Plc

# Contents

# THE QUEEN'S HOUSEHOLD

## THE LORD CHAMBERLAIN

| THE PRIVATE SECRETARY'S OFFICE | THE PRIVY PURSE & TREASURER'S OFFICE | THE LORD CHAMBERLAIN'S OFFICE | THE MASTER OF THE HOUSEHOLD'S DEPARTMENT | THE ROYAL MEWS DEPARTMENT | THE ROYAL COLLECTION DEPARTMENT |
|---|---|---|---|---|---|
| Private Secretary to The Queen | Keeper of the Privy Purse & Treasurer to The Queen | Comptroller | Master of the Household | Crown Equerry | Director of Royal Collection & Surveyor of The Queen's Works of Art |
| Assistant Private Secretaries | Deputy Keeper of the Privy Purse | Assistant Comptroller | Deputy Master of the Household | Administrators | Surveyor of The Queen's Pictures |
| Special Assistant | Assistant Keeper of the Privy Purse | Secretary | Assistants to the Master of the Household | Transport Officer | Librarian, The Royal Library, Windsor Castle |
| Policy & Research Officer | Chief Accountant & Paymaster | Assistant Secretary | Chief Clerk | Comptroller of Stores | Deputy Surveyor of The Queen's Works of Art |
| Chief Clerk | Personnel & Pensions Manager | State Invitations Assistant | Deputy to Assistant | Chief Clerk | Curator of the Print Room |
| Senior Correspondence Officer | Management Auditor | Registrar | Senior Clerk | Deputy Chief Clerk | Registrar |
| Secretary to the Private Secretary | Information Systems Manager | Clerks | Clerks | Office Keeper | Assistant to Registrar |
| Press Office | Deputy Chief Accountant | Permanent Lords in Waiting | Superintendent Windsor Castle | | Assistants to Surveyor of The Queen's Pictures |
| Communications Secretary | Senior Assistant Chief Accountant | Lords in Waiting | Assistant to Superintendent | | Inventory Assistant |
| Press Secretary to The Queen | Accountants | Gentlemen Ushers | Palace Steward | | Clerks |
| Assistant Press Secretaries | Clerks | Extra Gentlemen Ushers | Chief Housekeeper | | |
| | | Gentleman Usher to the Sword of State | | | |

**Information Officers**
- Regional Information Officer
- Website Editor

**Royal Travel Office**
- Director of Royal Travel
- Assistant Director
- Operations Manager, The Queen's Helicopter Flight
- Defence Services Secretary

**The Royal Archives**
- Keeper
- Assistant Keeper
- Registrar

**Property Section**
- Director of Property Services
- Director of Finance
- Financial Controller
- Accountant, Property Services
- Accountant
- Fire Protection & Health & Safety Manager
- Maintenance Manager, Buckingham Palace & Royal Mews
- Maintenance Manager, St James's Palace & Kensington Palace
- Maintenance Manager, Windsor Castle and Royal Mews, Hampton Court

**Royal Travel Financial Section**
- Director of Finance, Royal Travel
- Financial Controller, Royal Travel
- Accountant

**Royal Estates & Studs**
- Resident Factor, Balmoral
- Land Agent, Sandringham
- Manager, Royal Studs
- Deputy Ranger, Windsor Great Park
- Farm Manager, Windsor

- Gentleman Usher of the Black Rod
- Sergeants at Arms
- Marshal of the Diplomatic Corps
- Vice-Marshal
- Constable & Governor of Windsor Castle
- Keeper of the Jewel House, Tower of London
- Master of The Queen's Music
- Poet Laureate
- Bargemaster
- Keeper of the Swans
- Superintendent of the State Apartments, St James's Palace

**ASCOT OFFICE**
- Her Majesty's Representative at Ascot
- Secretary

**ECCLESIASTICAL HOUSEHOLD**

**CHAPELS ROYAL**

**MEDICAL HOUSEHOLD**

**CENTRAL CHANCERY OF THE ORDERS OF KNIGHTHOOD**

**THE HONOURABLE CORPS OF GENTLEMEN AT ARMS**

**THE QUEEN'S BODYGUARD OF THE YEOMAN OF THE GUARD**

# Introduction

Public interest in the British Royal Family is inexhaustible. Every detail of whatever they do, wear, eat and drink is avidly consumed; it is a never-ending soap opera to rival anything seen on our television screens. They are members of a highly privileged family, whose constitutional role and their place in the history of Britain creates enormous curiosity. Their private lives are lived in the main on the public stage with a cast of characters who may be straight out of the top drawer, but whose behaviour occasionally matches those in *EastEnders* or *Coronation Street*.

When Zara Philips, daughter of the Princess Royal, appeared with a stud showing through her pierced tongue (and another in her navel), it made headlines for days. Similarly, when one of the Duke of York's daughters was photographed on a beach topless, the pictures sold all over the world. Prince William's and Prince Harry's love-lives constantly feed the tabloids' gossip columnists, while speculation about the wealth of the Windsors provides endless stories in newspapers and magazines throughout the world.

During the Queen's reign, a succession of Royals has emerged to capture the public's attention with each generation developing its own particular newsworthy magic. The late Princess Margaret was the first of the truly glamorous royal women to attract media and public spotlight, not all of it favourable. Prince Charles, as a young man, was said to be the most eligible bachelor in the world for years – until he married an even more glamorous young woman, Lady Diana Spencer – who eclipsed him and became the most photographed woman in the world. Her tragic death in 1997 focussed a spotlight on Royalty that has yet to be dimmed. The Queen Mother, particularly during her widowhood that lasted 50 years, was among the most highly admired of royal personalities, who was awarded that most unwanted, embarrassing and dubious accolade, a 'National Treasure'.

Many myths have grown up surrounding Royalty and this books aims to examine most of them and to provide an insight into many of the lesser-known activities and practices of the Monarchy.

# The Royal Family

## The Queen

| | |
|---|---|
| **Title:** | Her Most Excellent Majesty Elizabeth the Second, by the Grace of God of the United Kingdom of Great Britain and Northern Ireland and of Her Other Realms and Territories Queen, Head of the Commonwealth, Defender of the Faith. |
| **Name:** | Elizabeth Alexandra Mary |
| **Date of birth:** | 21 April 1926 |
| **Parents:** | King George VI and Queen Elizabeth |
| **Sister:** | Princess Margaret Rose (21 August 1930 – 9 February 2002) |
| **Husband:** | His Royal Highness, the Duke of Edinburgh |
| **Married:** | 20 November 1947 at Westminster Abbey |
| **Acceded to the Throne:** | 6 February 1952 |
| **Children:** | HRH The Prince of Wales (14 November 1948) – Charles Philip Arthur George<br>HRH The Princess Royal (15 August 1950) – Anne Elizabeth Alice Louise<br>HRH The Duke of York (19 February 1960) – Andrew Albert Christian Edward<br>HRH The Earl of Wessex (10 March 1964) – Edward Antony Richard Louis |

Queen Elizabeth II is the 42nd Monarch of England but only its 6th Queen Regnant.

Her coronation took place in Westminster Abbey on 2 June 1953.

As Princess Elizabeth, she first rode on the London Underground in 1939 when she was 13 and did not travel by bus until she was 19.

In 1940, at the age of 14, she made her first broadcast.

In 1942, when she was 16, she took the salute for the first time as Colonel of the Grenadier Guards. In 1944, she was appointed a Counsellor of State. In 1945, she joined the Auxiliary Territorial Service (ATS) as a junior officer, but her father, King George VI, refused to allow her to sleep in the Officers' Mess and ordered her to return every night to Windsor Castle.

In 1947, on the morning of her wedding, a minor catastrophe was feared when the bride's bouquet could not be found. Eventually all was well when it was discovered in a refrigerator where a well-meaning footman had placed it.

Among her pioneering journeys was her first transatlantic flight to Canada in a BOAC airliner in 1951 in spite of warnings that it might be too dangerous.

## HRH The Duke of Edinburgh

| | |
|---|---|
| **Title:** | His Royal Highness, the Prince Philip, Duke of Edinburgh, Earl of Merioneth and Baron Greenwich |
| **Date of Birth:** | 10 June 1921 |
| **Place of Birth:** | Corfu, Greece |
| **Marriage:** | 20 November 1947 at Westminster Abbey |

**Children:** Charles, Anne, Andrew, Edward
**Service Rank:** Admiral of the Fleet, Royal Navy
**Honours:** Knight of the Garter, Knight of the Thistle, Privy Councillor, Order of Merit, Knight Grand Cross of the Order of the British Empire

Prince Philip of Greece, who although he claims not have a single drop of Greek blood in his veins, was born on the dining table of his parents' home, Mon Repos, on the Greek island of Corfu.

His father was Prince Andrew of Greece, a son of King George I of The Hellenes, who was, in fact, Danish.

Prince Philip's surname, which he never used, was Schleswig-Holstein-Sonderburg-Glucksberg.

Prince Philip and the Queen are third cousins as direct descendants of Queen Victoria.

Before he married Princess Elizabeth in 1947, Philip renounced his Greek citizenship and title and changed his religion from Greek Orthodox to Anglican. He also became a Freemason but was never an active member.

At the time of the wedding, King George VI allowed his new son-in-law to be styled HRH and also made him a Knight of the Garter, but a week later than his wife to remind him of her superior standing.

The Queen has showered her husband with honours, creating him a Prince of the United Kingdom in1957 and, in 1968, as a 47th birthday present, she awarded him the Order of Merit.

## HRH The Prince of Wales

**Title:** His Royal Highness, The Prince of Wales, Earl of Chester, Duke of Cornwall, Duke of Rothesay, Earl of Carrick, Baron of Renfrew, Lord of the Isles, Prince and Great Steward of Scotland.

**Date of Birth:** 14 November 1948, Buckingham Palace

**Christening:** 15 December 1948, the Music Room at Buckingham Palace

**Names:** Charles Philip Arthur George

**Honours:** Knight of the Garter (this Honour was granted automatically when Charles became Prince of Wales in 1958, but his installation did not take place until 1968), Knight of the Thistle (1977), Knight Grand Cross of the Order of the Bath (GCB 1975), Order of Merit (2002), Knight of the Order of Australia (AK 1981), Companion of the Queen's Service Order (QSO 1983), Privy Councillor (PC), Aide-de-Camp (ADC)

**Medals:** The Queen's Service Order (New Zealand 1983)
Coronation Medal (1953)
Silver Jubilee Medal (1977)
Golden Jubilee Medal (2002)
Canadian Forces Decoration (2002)
The New Zealand Commemorative Medal (1990)

**Marriage:** (1) Lady Diana Spencer, 29 July 1981, dissolved 28 August 1996
(2) Mrs Camilla Parker Bowles, 9 April 2006

**Children:** Prince William of Wales, 21 June 1982
Prince Henry of Wales, 15 September 1984

**Homes:** Clarence House, Highgrove, Birkhall

On the accession of his mother as Elizabeth II in 1952, Prince Charles became Heir Apparent and Duke of Cornwall. At the same time he inherited his Scottish titles.

Charles was educated at Hill House School in London, then Cheam Preparatory School in Berkshire, before going to his father's old public school Gordonstoun (which he hated, even though they made him Head Boy.) After A-levels he went up to Trinity College, Cambridge, from where he graduated with a 2.1 degree in Archaeology, Anthropology and History. He spent a term at the University of Wales, Aberystwyth, learning Welsh before his Investiture as Prince of Wales took place in Caernarvon Castle on 1 July 1969.

Between 1969 and 1977, Charles pursued a career in the Armed Forces, first of all serving in the RAF, where he qualified for his 'wings' as a pilot, before joining the Royal Navy where he eventually commanded his own ship, HMS Bronington.

When he was appointed Colonel-in-Chief of the Parachute Regiment, he successfully completed a parachute course and was awarded his 'brevet'.

His first marriage to Lady Diana Spencer in 1981 was seen by a worldwide television audience estimated to be over 500 million.

He is now associated with over 400 civilian and military organisations including The Bible Society, The Dry-Stone Walling Society, Beaufort Polo Club and Glamorgan County Cricket Club.

Prince Charles often exhibits his own paintings under the pseudonym 'Carrick' – taken from one of his subsidiary titles, Earl of Carrick.

## HRH Prince William of Wales, KG

| | |
|---|---|
| **Name:** | William Arthur Philip Louis |
| **Honours:** | Royal Knight Companion of the Order of the Garter (2008) |
| | Counsellor of State (1993) |
| | Honorary Commandant, Royal Air Force, Conningsby (2008) |
| **Date of Birth:** | 21 June 1982, Lindo Wing, St Mary's Hospital, Paddington, London |
| **Christening:** | 4 August 1982, Music Room, Buckingham Palace |
| **Godparents:** | King Constantine of The Hellenes, Sir Laurens van der Post, Lord Romsey, Princess Alexandra, The Duchess of Westminster, Lady Susan Hussey |

When William was born to Charles and Diana in 1982, he was the first child born to a Prince of Wales since 1905, when the future King George V, the Queen's grandfather, and his wife, Princess May of Teck (later Queen Mary), had the last of their six children, Prince John, who died at the age of 14.

William was born at 9.03pm on 21 June 1982 and weighed in at 7lbs 1½oz. The Archbishop of Canterbury, Dr Robert Runcie, officiated at his christening.

His education began at Mrs Jane Mynors' Nursery School in London, followed by Wetherby School, also in the capital. Then in September 1990, William attended Ludgrove School in Berkshire where he remained until 5 July 1995. Passing his Common Entrance examination, he became a pupil at Eton, at the insistence of the Queen and his mother, who did not want him to go to Gordonstoun. During his time at Eton, William would join his grandmother at Windsor Castle on Sunday afternoons where she gave him informal instruction in constitutional monarchy.

William was 15 years old when his mother, Diana, Princess

of Wales, died in 1997, and he and his younger bother, Harry, walked in the funeral procession with his grandfather, the Duke of Edinburgh, his father and his uncle Charles, Earl Spencer, to Westminster Abbey.

Before going to St Andrews University in Fife, where he graduated with a 2.1 degree in Geography, he took a gap year travelling in Belize, Chile and Africa.

Leaving St Andrews, William was enrolled as an officer cadet at Sandhurst, after passing the Regulations Commissions Board in October 2005 and, in December 2006, he was commissioned as a Second Lieutenant in the Household Cavalry (the Blues and Royals), the regiment of which his aunt, the Princess Royal, is Colonel-in-Chief. William was promoted to Lieutenant in December 2007 and, as part of his ongoing training as future Sovereign, he underwent an intensive flying course with the RAF, being awarded his pilot's 'wings' on 11 April 2008. In the RAF, he is known as Flight Lieutenant William Wales and, at the time of writing, he is training to be a Search and Rescue helicopter pilot, while still retaining his commission in the regular Army.

## HRH Prince Henry of Wales

**Name:** Henry Charles Albert David
**Date of Birth:** 15 September 1984, Lindo Wing, St Mary's Hospital, Paddington, London
**Christening:** 21 December 1984, St George's Chapel, Windsor, by Dr Robert Runcie, Archbishop of Canterbury
**Godparents:** Prince Andrew (now Duke of York), Lady Sarah Armstrong Jones (now Lady Sarah Chatto), Lady Cecce Vestey, Mrs William Bartholomew (formerly Caroline Pride), Mr Bryan Organ

Prince Henry, known to everyone, including all the Royal Family, as Harry, was born third in Line of Succession to the Throne, but if and when his brother marries and has children, they will take precedence and he will move down the line.

His early education followed exactly that of his brother, William: Mrs Mynors' Nursery, Wetherby and Eton, where he gained A-levels in Art and Geography.

To mark his 18th birthday in 2002, the Queen gave him his own Coat of Arms.

His gap year was spent in Australia and Africa and, in May 2005, having passed the Regular Commissions Board (RCB) in September the previous year, Harry entered the Royal Military Academy at Sandhurst. On 12 April 2006, he was commissioned into the Household Cavalry, and saw action in Afghanistan for two months until early 2008. He trained as a helicopter pilot with the Army Air Corps and, while continuing his military career; he is also associated with a number of charities including one that supports children orphaned by AIDS in Lesotho, where Harry had spent part of his gap year.

## HRH The Duchess of Cornwall

Born Camilla Rosemary Shand on 17 July 1947 at King's College Hospital, London, the Duchess is the eldest of three children, with a sister, Annabel Elliot (née Shand) and a brother, Mark Shand. Their father was Major Bruce Shand who died in June 2006.

The Duchess's first marriage was to Brigadier Andrew Parker Bowles of the Blues and Royals, on 4 July 1973, at the Guards Chapel, Wellington Barracks. A Roman Catholic priest conducted the service as the groom was a Catholic, but Camilla was never required to convert. She remained an Anglican.

Two children – Thomas Henry (Tom) (1974), and Laura Rose (1978) – were born and the marriage was dissolved in 1995. The Duchess and her former husband are now grandparents.

The Prince of Wales and Mrs Parker Bowles were married in a civil ceremony on 9 April 2005 at The Guildhall, Windsor, followed by a service of Prayer and Dedication in St George's Chapel, Windsor Castle, conducted by Dr Rowan Williams, Archbishop of Canterbury, and afterwards the Queen gave a reception for the couple.

At the time of the marriage, it was announced that Prince Charles's wife would be known as the Duchess of Cornwall, one of his subsidiary titles, not the Princess of Wales, to which she is legally entitled. She is known in Scotland as the Duchess of Rothesay and another of her titles is Countess of Chester. When Prince Charles becomes King, his wife will be known as Princess Consort.

Her Royal Highness is involved with a number of charities, including the Osteoporosis Society, of which she is Patron, and she is also associated with several regiments and other military units.

## HRH The Duke of York, KG KCVO

| | |
|---|---|
| **Name:** | Andrew Albert Christian Edward |
| **Titles:** | His Royal Highness The Duke of York, Royal Knight Companion of the Most Noble Order of the Garter, Knight Commander of the Royal Victorian Order, Earl of Inverness, Baron Killyleagh |
| **Date of Birth:** | 19 February 1960, Buckingham Palace |
| **Medals and decorations:** | Silver Jubilee Medal, 1977 South Atlantic Campaign Medal, 1982 New Zealand Commemoration Medal, 1990 Canadian Decoration, 2001 |
| **Marriage:** | Miss Sarah Ferguson, 23 July 1985 at Westminster Abbey; dissolved May 1996 |

When Prince Andrew was born in 1960, he was the first child born to a reigning Monarch in 103 years, since Princess Beatrice, daughter of Queen Victoria, had since been born in April 1857.

A governess at home taught Andrew initially, and then when he was 8, he was sent to Heatherdown Preparatory School in Ascot, where he remained until he was 13. At that time, he was enrolled at Gordonstoun, just like his older brother and father.

He passed his O-level examinations and, to broaden his outlook, he travelled to Canada in 1977, completing two terms at Lakefield College in Ontario.

Back at Gordonstoun for his A-levels, Andrew passed in four subjects and then travelled to France and Germany to improve his languages.

The Royal Navy was always going to be his choice of service for a career and he followed his father to the Royal Naval College at Dartmouth until he was commissioned in 1980, serving for 22 years as a helicopter pilot before he left to become the UK's Special Representative for International Trade and Investment. During his naval career, Andrew saw active service in the Falklands in 1982 flying a Sea King helicopter from *HMS Invincible*.

On 19 March 1986, Prince Andrew became engaged to Sarah Ferguson (born 15 October 1959), the second daughter of Major Ronald Ferguson and Susan, the late Mrs Hector Barrantes. They were married in Westminster Abbey on 23 July 1985 and, at the time of their marriage, Andrew was created Duke of York, with his wife becoming Duchess.

Two daughters, Beatrice Elizabeth Mary (8 August 1988) and Eugenie Victoria Helena (23 May 1990) were born, both at the Portland Hospital in London and, in May 1996, Andrew and Sarah divorced. Neither has yet remarried. At the time of the divorce, the Queen announced that Sarah would not retain her title of Her Royal Highness. She is simply known as the Duchess of York.

The Duke of York carries out a wide range of public duties and he is linked to over 100 organisations, ranging from charities concerned with the deaf to the Patronage of the English National Ballet, a role he assumed following the death of its previous Patron, the Princess of Wales.

His Royal Highness is passionate about golf and sailing, and he has retained his interest in flying as President of the Royal Aero Club of Great Britain since 1982.

His current home is Royal Lodge, Windsor, a residence he has occupied since the death of the former tenant, his grandmother, Queen Elizabeth, the Queen Mother.

## HRH Prince Edward, Earl of Wessex, KG, KCVO

**Name:**          Edward Antony Richard Louis
**Date of Birth:**  10 March 1964, Buckingham Palace
**Marriage:**      Miss Sophie Rhys-Jones, 19 June 1999,
                   Westminster Abbey

**Medals and decorations:** Silver Jubilee Medal (1977)
Golden Jubilee Medal (2002)
New Zealand Commemorative Medal (1990)
Commander of the Royal Victorian Order (CVO), (1989)
Knight Commander of the Royal Victorian Order (KCVO), (2003)
Knight Companion of the Most Noble Order of the Garter (KG), (2006)

HRH Prince Edward was christened in the Private Chapel at Windsor Castle and his early life followed that of his siblings. He underwent private tuition until he was seven when he went to Gibbs Pre-Preparatory School in Kensington and then on to Heatherdown in Ascot in 1972.

1977 saw him being enrolled at Gordonstoun, where he was elected Guardian (Head Boy) for his final term. He was successful in his A-levels in History, English Literature, Economics and Political Studies. Edward left Gordonstoun in 1982 and travelled to New Zealand where he taught for two terms at the Collegiate School in Wanganui.

Returning to Britain, he became a student at Jesus College, Cambridge, leaving with a BA in 1986. It was while he was at Cambridge that he joined the Royal Marines as a University Cadet, but he failed to complete a Commando training course at Lympstone in Dorset and resigned from the Royal Marines.

For nearly ten years he pursued a career in the theatre, working for Andrew (now Lord) Lloyd Webber and later running his own company, Ardent Productions.

Prince Edward and Sophie Rhys-Jones announced their engagement on 6 January 1999 and were married at St George's Chapel, Windsor that same year on 19 June.

The Prince was created Earl of Wessex on his marriage, with

his bride becoming HRH The Countess of Wessex. It was also announced at the same time that eventually Edward would become Duke of Edinburgh when the title once more reverts to the Crown.

Sophie had been born in Oxford on 20 January 1965 and educated at Dulwich College Preparatory School and Kent College School for Girls, before embarking on a career in public relations.

The couple have two children, Lady Louise, born 8 November 2003; and James, born 17 December 2007. James has been given his father's subsidiary title of Viscount Severn.

Both the Earl and Countess are involved in royal duties, with Edward playing an active role in the Duke of Edinburgh's Award Scheme. They also work on behalf of a number of charities and organisations, especially those concerned with young people, the arts and sport. Their home is the magnificent Bagshot Park, said to be one of the grandest of all Royal residences.

## HRH The Princess Royal

| | |
|---|---|
| **Title:** | Her Royal Highness The Princess Royal, KG, KT, GCVO, Mrs Timothy Laurence |
| **Name:** | Anne Elizabeth Alice Louise |
| **Date of Birth:** | 15 August 1950, Clarence House |
| **Marriage:** | (1) Mark Phillips, 14 November 1973, Westminster Abbey; dissolved April 1992 (2) Timothy Laurence, 12 December 1992, Crathie Church, Balmoral |

| | |
|---|---|
| **Children:** | Peter Mark Andrew Phillips, 15 November 1977 |
| | Zara Anne Elizabeth Phillips, 15 May 1981 |
| **Medals and Decorations:** | Dame Grand Cross of the Royal Victorian Order (GCVO), (1974) |
| | Knight of the Most Noble Order of the Garter (KG), (1994) |
| | Knight of the Most Noble Order of the Thistle (KT), (2001) |

If ever a royal princess could be said to have ushered in the second half of a century, it must surely be Princess Anne. She was born ten minutes before noon on 15 August 1950, and weighed in at exactly 6lbs.

Within minutes, a bulletin was issued from Clarence House:

*'Her Royal Highness the Princess Elizabeth, Duchess of Edinburgh, was safely delivered of a Princess at 11.50am today. Her Royal Highness and her daughter are doing well.'*

Like her brothers before her, Anne began her education privately at Buckingham Palace (she was two when her mother acceded to the Throne) and then she left to become a boarder at Benenden girls' school in Kent. She made a personal decision not to go on to university and started her public career at the age of 18. In 1970, she became President of the Save the Children Fund for whom she has worked continuously ever since.

Princess Anne won the individual European Three-Day Event championship in 1971, and became the BBC Sports Personality of the Year. Competing as part of the British team in the European championships in Germany in 1975, she won silver medals both individually and in the team event. The Princess also took part in the 1976 Montreal Olympic Games, where she was severely concussed after her horse fell on the Cross Country Course.

An expert and highly competitive horsewoman, she married a fellow equestrian, Lieutenant Mark Phillips of 1st The Queen's Dragoon Guards, at Westminster Abbey on 14 November 1973 and, four months later, an attempt was made by an armed man to kidnap her within sight of Buckingham Palace. She was unharmed, but her personal protection officer, James Beaton, was shot five times. He was awarded the George Cross for his bravery in preventing the kidnap attempt.

The Princess and Mark Phillips had two children: Peter, born in 1977, followed by Zara in 1981.

Zara has more than emulated her mother's achievements by winning both the European and World Three-Day Event championships.

Neither of the children has a title, on their mother's insistence, although in 1987, she did accept the title of Princess Royal for herself.

Princess Anne and Mark Phillips divorced in 1992, and a second marriage to one of her mother's equerries, Tim Laurence, followed that same year. The couple live at Gatcombe Park in Gloucestershire.

In 1986, the Princess succeeded the Duke of Edinburgh as President of the Fédération Equestre Internationale (FEI), a post she has since relinquished, and she is also an active President of the British Olympic Association. Riding for the Disabled is another of her interests and she has been their President since 1969.

The Princess Royal is President or Patron of some 320 organisations, plus many military, Royal Air Force and naval units. Although she travels to many parts of the world supporting her charities, she does not court personal publicity; in her own words, 'I do not do stunts.' One of the volunteer workers at Save the Children said she has an air of confidence and caring – a rare combination in an increasingly cynical world. She also regularly tops the 'league table' in the number of Royal duties carried out.

## Diana, Princess of Wales (1961–97)

**Name:** Diana Frances Spencer
**Date of Birth:** 1 July 1961, Park House, Sandringham Estate, Norfolk
**Death:** 31 August 1997, Paris
**Marriage:** 29 July 1981, St Paul's Cathedral; dissolved 28 August 1996
**Children:** Prince William of Wales (William Arthur Philip Louis), 21 June 1982
Prince Henry (Harry) of Wales (Henry Charles Albert David), 15 September 1984

The Princess of Wales was not royal by birth, although her family had descended from Henry VII.

Diana was born on the Sandringham Estate on 1 July 1961 as her father, then Viscount Althorp, had rented Park House from the Queen to whom he was Equerry (1950–54), as he had been to her father King George VI (1950–52). Diana was the Honourable, not Lady, Diana Spencer, when she born; that title did not apply until her father succeeded to the Earldom in 1975, and the family moved to the stately home at Althorp in Northamptonshire.

Diana had two older sisters, Sarah and Jane, and a younger brother, Charles. There was also another brother called John, born in 1960, who survived only ten hours.

When Diana was just seven years old, her parents (her mother was the Hon Frances Roche, daughter of Baron Fermoy) divorced, with her father later marrying Raine, Countess of Dartmouth, the daughter of the novelist Barbara Cartland, and her mother marrying Peter Shand-Kydd.

Diana began her education at Riddlesworth Preparatory School in Norfolk, until, in 1974, she was sent as a boarder to West Heath in Kent. Leaving in 1977, Diana followed the usual path of girls of her station, being despatched to a finishing school – Institute Alpin

Videmanette in Rougemont, Switzerland – where she studied domestic science, typing and correspondence.

Returning to Britain, she worked as an assistant teacher at the Young England Kindergarten School in Pimlico, London, where she was first photographed in a see-through skirt that was seen in newspapers throughout the world, as word of her involvement with the Prince of Wales became public knowledge.

Once her engagement to Prince Charles had been announced, Diana moved into Clarence House under the protective wing of the Queen Mother and Diana's grandmother, Lady Fermoy, one of Her Majesty's Ladies-in-Waiting. The wedding took place on 29 July 1981, just a month after the bride's twentieth birthday. Prince Charles was nearly 12 years older.

In 1992, Diana and Charles's marriage collapsed, followed by divorce in 1996 when Diana had the title of Her Royal Highness removed; henceforth, she was known simply as Diana, Princess of Wales.

She continued her charitable works, concentrating on the homeless, disabled people and those suffering with HIV/AIDS and, in the year before her death, she campaigned vigorously for an end to the manufacture and use of land mines.

Diana died in a car crash in a Paris underpass on 31 August 1997, along with Dodi Fayed, son of the owner of Harrods. Few events in British history have produced more scenes of national grief and bewilderment and the funeral was described as an inspiring combination of traditional ritual and informality, with Royalty, statesmen and women from all over the world, film stars and showbusiness celebrities all anxious to mourn the young princess.

Diana's body was laid to rest at her childhood home, Althorp, on a peaceful and secluded island in the middle of a lake.

# Royal Residences

## Buckingham Palace

Buckingham Palace is, without doubt, the most famous address in the world and is the official London residence of the Sovereign. It is the only royal residence to bear the name of its original owner, John Sheffield, Duke of Buckingham, who was persuaded to sell it to George III in 1762 for £28,000. It was not intended to be the main residence of the Monarch, and was called The Queen's House because the King wanted his wife, Queen Charlotte, to be provided with a private family home away from the formal Court at St James's. Fourteen of Queen Charlotte's fifteen children were born there.

Foreign emissaries are still accredited to the Court of St James's, not Buckingham Palace. Indeed, it wasn't until Queen Victoria came to the Throne in 1837 that the Palace became the official London residence of the Sovereign, and it has remained so ever since. None of the Monarchs who have lived there has particularly liked the place; Edward VII, who moved in in 1902, detested it; George V also disliked it intensely, saying, 'Buckingham Palace is just a house; Sandringham is a home...'; Edward VIII, the King who was never crowned, installed extra bathrooms and even a shower, but stayed away from the place whenever he could; and King George VI had to be persuaded by no less a figure than Winston Churchill to live in Buckingham Palace when he acceded to the Throne in 1937, and he never concealed his dislike of its museum-like interior. Elizabeth II has always said that Windsor Castle is her favourite home.

Buckingham Palace currently has: 19 State Apartments; 52 royal and guest bedrooms; 188 staff bedrooms; 78 bathrooms and lavatories; 92 offices used by the Royal Household; its own post office, telephone exchange and police station. The cellars of the Palace contain more than 1,000 bottles of vintage champagne.

The priceless gold plate used at State Banquets is kept in a locked, fortified strongroom in the basement. A Palace legend is that a footman was once discovered blind drunk in the strongroom, draped in some of the gold plate. Apparently, his major crime was that he had drunk a bottle of brandy worth thousands of pounds.

Although the Palace refuses to confirm or deny it, there is a subterranean passage that can be opened on to the Piccadilly Underground line that connects directly with Heathrow Airport, and which could be used to evacuate the Royal Family in an emergency.

A reinforced and fully equipped bunker in the basement is said to be capable of withstanding a nuclear attack.

Buckingham Palace was bombed nine times during the Second World War including: 1940 (the Chapel Royal was destroyed); 1941 (bombs fell in the Forecourt and on North Lodge); 1944 (a V1 landed in the garden – no one was injured).

The palace also boasts a swimming pool (see Swimming) and a squash court and the Palace is surrounded by a 45-acre garden that contains a 4-acre lake, where Prince Charles and Princess Anne, when they were young, were taught how to row.

The largest of the State Apartments is the Ballroom: 123 feet long, 60 feet wide and 45 feet high, said to be the largest private ballroom in Britain and was commissioned by Queen Victoria at a cost of £250,000 (£25 million at today's prices). It was opened on 17 June 1856 with a grand ball to celebrate the end of the Crimean War. Today, it is used more than 20 times a year as the venue for Investitures (see Investitures).

The Queen and Prince Philip's private apartments are located on the first floor of the North Wing, facing Constitution Hill (Charles II used to take his constitutional walks there), with Her Majesty's rooms being the only ones with bow windows.

On 9 July 1982, Michael Fagan, a 31-year-old schizophrenic, entered the Palace at 7.00am and found his way into the Queen's bedroom. She woke to find him sitting on her bed, bleeding from a cut thumb. Her personal police officer, who sits outside her door all night, had left to have a cup of tea, and no one answered Her Majesty's 'panic button'. It was only when her maid and footman entered that they managed to bundle Fagan into a cupboard and overpower him. Fagan later spent some time in a mental institution and was eventually released.

It is now possible for anyone to see around Buckingham Palace as the Queen agreed to open the building and grounds to the public, with the first visitors being admitted on 7 August 1993. The Palace opens every year during August and September, when the Queen is away at Balmoral (see Balmoral) and, as well as viewing all the State Apartments, with audio guides in several languages, visitors can also use the shop in the gardens where souvenirs are sold.

As a working building, Buckingham Palace houses the offices of the main departments of the Royal Household, including: The Lord Chamberlain's Office; The Queen's Private Secretary; The Keeper of the Privy Purse; the Press Office; and the Master of the Household (see Royal Household). The Royal Mews (Stables and Garages), situated at the far end of the Palace Gardens, are entered via Buckingham Palace Road while the Royal Collection is based across the road in St James's Palace.

An intriguing fact about the appearance of Buckingham Palace is that from the front it never changes, summer or winter. The windows are never opened, no matter how warm the day is, and the net curtains are never drawn back in order to preserve the pristine 'chocolate box' effect of this famous London landmark.

## Windsor Castle

Windsor is the oldest continuously occupied castle and fortress in Europe with the present castle used as a residence by every Monarch since William the Conqueror built a fortified mound around the Keep to be used as a headquarters for hunting.

Subsequent Monarchs have added to and modernised the castle, which was used as a military base and prison during the Civil War.

Charles II redesigned many of the State Apartments including St George's Hall (destroyed by fire in 1992 and brilliantly reconstructed) and it was also Charles II who set out the Long Walk through Windsor Great Park towards Ascot.

Queen Victoria loved the castle and she proposed to Prince Albert there. It was also where he died on 14 December 1861, after which Her Majesty became known as 'The Widow of Windsor'.

The Queen spends every weekend at Windsor, arriving at the Sovereign's Entrance, and the Court moves there for one week during April.

The castle is surrounded by an estate of 4,800 acres known as Windsor Great Park that has a public road running through it linking Windsor and Ascot. Except on this road, no cars are allowed in the Park. The Long Walk is open to the public but only if they are on foot or in horse-drawn carriages.

The Castle is open to the public all year round from 10.00am to 5.00pm (4.00pm in winter) and the bookshops in the Lower and Middle Wards stock many items relating to Royalty.

The fire that damaged much of Windsor Castle in 1992 began in the Queen's Private Chapel and the restoration was completed in November 1997.

In 1999, Prince Edward married Sophie Rhys- Jones in St George's Chapel.

In 2002, Queen Elizabeth, the Queen Mother was interred in the tomb of her husband, King George VI.

In April 2006, a service of blessing was held in St George's Chapel for Prince Charles and the Duchess of Cornwall, after their civil marriage in Windsor's Town Hall.

**Frogmore House and Mausoleum**
One of the most beautiful and certainly most tranquil of all royal homes, though now unoccupied, is Frogmore House, located in Windsor Home Park which is the private part of the Windsor Estate. The house was a great favourite of Queen Victoria and both she and Prince Albert are buried in the Frogmore Mausoleum that stands in the grounds.

Frogmore was opened to the public for the first time in August 1990. The current opening times are from the second week in August to the end of September.

Admission prices are: Adults – £7; Seniors and Students –

£6; Under 17s – £5.

The Mausoleums are open only on the Wednesday nearest to 24 May (Queen Victoria's birthday) and on the first Wednesday and Thursday in May.

To the south of the Mausoleums lies the Frogmore Royal Burial Ground, where members of the Royal Family, but not the Sovereign, are interred. This area is not open to the public at any time, but an information board indicates who is buried there. Included are the Duke of Windsor (previously King Edward VIII) who died in 1972, and his Duchess, the former Mrs Wallis Simpson, who died in 1986.

Among those who have lived or stayed at Frogmore are Queen Victoria's mother, the Duchess of Kent, and Queen Alexandra, who, when she was still Princess of Wales, gave birth to her elder son, Prince Albert Victor, later the Duke of Clarence, in 1864.

In 1900, the future Earl Mountbatten of Burma was born in the house and, from 1902–10, the Duke of York (later King George V) and his wife loved to spend holidays there with their children.

In 1923, another Duke and Duchess of York (later King George VI and Queen Elizabeth) spent part of their honeymoon at Frogmore. They were the last members of the Royal Family to use Frogmore as a residence but today receptions are frequently held in its elegant rooms.

## St James's Palace

No Royal palace, in England or Scotland, has as strange and sinister an origin as St James's Palace. It was built on the site of what was once a hospital for female lepers (the Hospital of St James, Westminster, hence the name) until it was bought by no less a figure than Henry VIII in 1532, from the Provost of Eton College. It took eight years for the Palace to be completed and for 300 years it was lived in by English sovereigns and became the official London residence of the Monarch in 1702, when Queen Anne was forced to move the Court to St James's following a fire at Whitehall Palace. It has remained so to this day, even though many people believe that Buckingham Palace occupies that role. In fact, William IV was the last Monarch to live in St James's and, on her accession in 1837, Queen Victoria moved into Buckingham Palace. However, St James's remains the senior palace of the Sovereign, and it is to St James's that all foreign ambassadors and high commissioners are accredited, even though they present their letters of credence to the Queen at Buckingham Palace.

Members of the Royal Household are also housed inside the Palace environs, including the Marshal of the Diplomatic Corps, who lives in the splendid, four-storey Tudor Gatehouse complete with its original Henry VIII cypher; the house faces up St James's Street and guards stand on sentry duty 24 hours a day.

Today, the only royal inhabitants of St James's are the Princess Royal, who has an apartment in York House (part of the Palace); the Duke of Kent; his sister, Princess Alexandra; and the most recent tenant, Princess Beatrice, daughter of the Duke of York, who has taken over an apartment while she is a student at Goldsmiths College.

The accession of a new Monarch is proclaimed from the Brick Balcony overlooking Friary Court in St James's Palace, and visiting Heads of State use the State Apartments to hold receptions. The Palace is divided into four Courts: Engine Court, Ambassadors Court, Friary Court and Colour Court. There are still remnants of

Henry VIII's Tudor building including the Chapel Royal, where Queen Victoria was married in 1840 and two of the State Apartments are in their original condition.

Her Majesty allows certain charities to hold social functions in the State Apartments and royal wedding presents are traditionally displayed here with the proceeds going to charity. Otherwise, the Palace is not usually open to the public, but there is a guard mounting in Friary Court every morning that can be viewed from Marlborough Road.

Among the Royal Household offices located at St James's Palace are the Headquarters of the Yeomen of the Guard (see Yeomen of the Guard), Central Chancery of the Orders of Knighthood, the Ascot Office (see Ascot Office), the Marshal of the Diplomatic Corps and, in Stable Yard, the Royal Collection.

1840 – Queen Victoria married Prince Albert in the Chapel Royal, St James's Palace.
1997 – The coffin of Diana, Princess of Wales lay in front of the altar before her funeral at Westminster Abbey.

## Balmoral Castle

The Royal Family has always had a love affair with the Scottish Highlands ever since Queen Victoria and Prince Albert made their first visit to the area in 1842 and then bought Balmoral Castle and the surrounding estate of some 11,000 acres in 1852 for £31,000. They added several parcels of land so that today the Castle lies in over 50,000 acres of grounds and woodland, with the entire estate said to be worth currently over £50 million.

It is privately owned by the Queen and is not therefore a Crown property. If she wanted she could sell it at any time, but the convention is that, like Sandringham (see Sandringham), these houses are passed from generation to generation.

The Queen spends all of August and September and the first week in October at Balmoral where one of her favourite daily pastimes is to catch the bats that haunt the upper reaches of the great hall. She does this with the aid of a footman, and a large net attached to a long pole. The bats, which are a protected species, are then released, returning the following night to the castle. The Queen then repeats the exercise the next day.

The interior of the Castle is almost entirely Scottish in design with tartan very much in evidence: carpets, curtains and even wallpaper.

The late Harold Wilson, who visited when he was Prime Minister, said the place was locked in a time warp, 'like something out of *Brigadoon*', a reference to the Hollywood film depicting a fictional Scottish village.

The Queen's grandfather, King George V, opened the Castle gardens and grounds to the public in 1931 twice a week during the summer months. Now they are open from 10.00am to 5.00pm every weekday from 1 May to 31 July, but not during August and September when the Queen is in residence. There are three souvenir shops and a cafeteria, plus a fascinating exhibition of royal carriages in the stables and, inside the Castle, the Ballroom displays examples of Her Majesty's collection of works of art.

As soon as the Royal Family arrive at Balmoral, they 'go native' in that they invariably wear tartan (see Tartan) and kilts, visit the Braemar Highland Games and hold Scottish country dances in the Ballroom.

Among the large houses on the Balmoral Estate are Birkhall (see Birkhall) and Craigowan (see Craigowan).

The Duke of Edinburgh is responsible for the running of Balmoral and its extensive estate, the sporting facilities (shooting rights are let out on a commercial basis with the going rate for stalking and killing a stag being £20,000, while the River Dee which runs through the estate is said to be among the best rivers in the country for salmon fishing).

A resident factor looks after the day-to-day administration, sending a monthly report directly to the Queen, while the Prince of Wales is also actively involved in the management and spends part of every summer at Birkhall.

## Birkhall

Birkhall is part of the Balmoral Estate, situated above the river Muick, and is the summer home of the Prince of Wales and the Duchess of Cornwall. It is still part of the Queen's private property and Prince Charles is merely the tenant, as was his late grandmother, Queen Elizabeth, the Queen Mother, who used the house for 50 years after she was widowed in 1952. Her Majesty loved the house as it was there that she and her husband when he was Duke of York (later King George VI) stayed in the early 1930s.

Birkhall was originally built in 1715 and came into the possession of the Royal Family when Queen Victoria bought it in 1849. It was intended to be used by the then Prince of Wales (later Edward VII) who did not stay there until 1862 when he indicated that he preferred nearby Abergeldie, which he took on a long lease.

In 1856, the house received one of its most distinguished visitors when Florence Nightingale stayed briefly as the guest of the then tenant, Sir James Clark, the Queen's Physician.

Prince Charles took over the tenancy on the death of his grandmother in 2001, and he has spent considerable amounts of private money improving the house and grounds.

## Hampton Court Palace

Hampton Court Palace, standing on the banks of the River Thames just 15 miles south-west of London, was once the largest private residence in England. Originally built for Cardinal Wolsey in 1514, it is the most sumptuous of all royal palaces in both size and splendour.

The Cardinal gave the palace to Henry VIII in an ill-judged attempt to regain the favour he had lost, but it was to no avail and, in 1529, the Crown seized all his land and possessions. It still belongs to the Queen in right of the Crown but, since 1989, it has been one of the five palaces managed by the Historic Royal Palaces Agency. It was once a favourite residence for Royalty and even used on occasion for honeymoons.

Charles I was kept prisoner at Hampton Court after the Civil War, and his captor, Oliver Cromwell, lived there in some style as Lord Protector. When the Monarchy was restored, Charles II spent a great deal of money refurbishing the Palace and gardens and Queen Anne continued the restoration when she ascended the throne.

The last Sovereign to live at Hampton Court was George II (1727–60).

Today, the Palace is open to the public and its State Apartments can be hired for commercial and private use, while the annual Hampton Court Flower Show is regarded as a rival to Chelsea.

The Palace is surrounded by a royal deer park of 615 acres and is a popular spot for local visitors and tourists to enjoy its wildlife and the trees, some of which are said to be over 450 years old.

## Kensington Palace

Kensington Palace was once described by Prince Charles as the 'aunt heap' because so many of his elderly relatives lived there in the collection of flats and apartments, all of which are on loan from the Queen as 'grace and favour' homes. The number of Royal relations still living in the Palace has been greatly reduced with the deaths of Princess Alice, Duchess of Gloucester, Princess Margaret and Diana, Princess of Wales; now, the Duke and Duchess of Gloucester and Prince and Princess Michael of Kent are the only remaining Royals in residence.

William III (1689–1702) bought Kensington Palace from the Earl of Nottingham for 18,000 guineas in 1689 – a considerable sum in those days.

William III bought the property because Whitehall Palace was prone to flooding and Hampton Court Palace was considered to be too far out of central London. During the next five years, William spent a further £101,000 on extending and refurbishing the Palace before he was satisfied.

William III died in Kensington Palace after he ordered his servants to carry him from Hampton Court Palace after a serious riding accident.

Kensington Palace is today remembered mainly as the place where Queen Victoria was born in 1819, and where she received the news that she was Queen in 1837 on the death of her uncle, William IV. The Court actually sat at Kensington Palace for three weeks before Victoria moved to Buckingham Palace, which became her principal residence.

This was the last time Kensington Palace was used as an

official residence by a Sovereign and today the magnificent State Apartments, maintained in their original splendour, are open to the public all year round. Exhibitions are held showing different aspects of royal life through the ages and the present occupants of the 'grace and favour' homes are not inconvenienced by the hordes of visitors as their homes are well protected and screened on the west side of the building.

## Sandringham

120 miles from London, in the Norfolk countryside, stands a large, not very attractive house made of red brick with a grey slate roof. It is one of the Queen's favourite homes, where she now spends Christmas (see Christmas) since the extended family has grown up, so Windsor Castle is no longer needed.

Sandringham House is a private dwelling owned outright by the Queen and left to her by her father. Queen Victoria bought it originally for £220,000 for her eldest son, later King Edward VII, and today stands in an estate of over 20,000 acres making the entire property worth in excess of £70 million.

Architecturally uninspired, the house is a typical example of the rather pretentious style enjoyed by many wealthy Victorians. The Queen's father, King George VI, considered it his favourite home, having been born there and dying there on 6 February 1952.

At one time, there were over 400 rooms at Sandringham but the Queen demolished 91 of them in 1965 as an economy move – and because they were rarely used.

Her Majesty farms some 3,000 acres of the estate with the remainder let to tenant farmers.

Among the houses on the Sandringham estate are Park House where the late Diana, Princess of Wales was born during the period when her father Viscount (later Earl) Spencer was

Equerry to the Queen, and York House, where King George V and Queen Mary (as Duke and Duchess of York) lived in great contentment for some years.

As with Balmoral Castle, much of the area surrounding Sandringham is open to the public and Her Majesty and the Royal Family attend morning service at the local parish church of St Mary Magdalene every Sunday when she is in residence.

## Clarence House

This is the last private house in The Mall and is currently occupied by the Prince of Wales and the Duchess of Cornwall. Princes William and Harry also have accommodation there.

The house was built in 1828 by John Nash (who also designed Regent Street) for the Duke of Clarence (later William IV). Another royal resident was Queen Victoria's mother, the Duchess of Kent, who lived there until she died in 1861.

During the Second World War, the house was used by the Red Cross and, in 1947, it became the first home of the then Princess Elizabeth and Prince Philip, who remained there until the Princess became Elizabeth II in 1952 and they moved across the road to Buckingham Palace. Princess Anne was born in Clarence House on 15 August 1950.

Queen Elizabeth, the Queen Mother was its next tenant (in 1953) and lived there for the rest of her life. On her death, her grandson, Prince Charles, moved in and the house has become not only his London home, but also the headquarters for his many activities. Some of the apartments at Clarence House are open to the public (admission fee) during the summer months.

If it came on the open market, experts have estimated the value of Clarence House to be well in excess of £70 million.

## Highgrove House

The Prince of Wales's country home in Gloucestershire was built in 1796, and then redesigned in 1894. Prince Charles bought it for an undisclosed sum in 1981 on his marriage to Lady Diana Spencer, partly because of its location and also because there was a 1,000-acre estate attached so he could develop his passion for gardening and also make use of the Home Farm for organic crops. Today, the farm is highly profitable with its products sold under the name 'Duchy Originals'.

Highgrove is not open to the public but His Royal Highness allows special parties to visit the gardens when he sometimes gives talks about his plants, particularly his wild flowers.

The Duchess of Cornwall also has her own 'bolt-hole' at Raymill House near Laycock where she and her children occasionally stay.

## Gatcombe Park

Close to Highgrove is Gatcombe Park, the home of the Princess Royal and her second husband, Vice-Admiral Timothy Laurence. The Queen bought it for the Princess and her first husband, Mark Phillips, for a sum believed to be around £500,000. Today, it would be worth £4–5 million.

After the Princess and Mark Phillips divorced, and both remarried, he went to live at nearby Aston Farm, again bought by the Queen and rented to him.

Gatcombe is a well-established horse trials venue, with the Cross

Country Course designed by Mark, who also collaborates with his ex-wife in organising commercial shoots on the estate.

## Royal Lodge

Situated in Windsor Great Park, Royal Lodge is an elegant country house that has replaced the original 18th-century brick property built in the Queen Anne style. Different generations of Royalty have lived there and made many alterations, including the Duke of Cumberland, the Prince Regent (in 1811) who also, when he became King George IV in 1820, changed the name of the house from King's Lodge to Royal Lodge.

William IV demolished part of Royal Lodge and, for 60 years, senior members of the Royal Household used it mainly as a 'grace and favour' home.

In 1931, King George V gave permission for his son, Prince Albert, the Duke of York, and his wife to take over the property and they moved in the following year, using Royal Lodge as a private country house, even after the Duke and Duchess became King George VI and Queen Elizabeth. They loved the place so much that, after His Majesty's death in 1952, his widow continued to live at weekends at Royal Lodge, until she died in 2002. Since then, her grandson, the present Duke of York, has occupied the Lodge and his daughters, Princesses Beatrice and Eugenie, love the place as much as he does.

The gardens reflect the character of the late Queen Mother, who spent many hours working there.

Also in the grounds are Y Bwthyn Bach (see Y Bwthyn Bach) and the Royal Chapel of All Saints.

## Osborne House

Queen Victoria and Prince Albert were looking for somewhere not too far from London or Windsor, but sufficiently distant from the formalities of the Court, to enable them to escape from the restrictions of their everyday life. The Isle of Wight in the Solent provided the ideal answer.

Her Majesty bought Osborne House at East Cowes from Lady Isabella Blachford in 1845 and, for the next five years, they changed the appearance and size of the property to accommodate their family. The Queen and her Consort divided their spare time, when not at Buckingham Palace or Windsor Castle, between Balmoral and Osborne, and when Prince Albert died at Windsor in 1861, his widow retreated to Osborne, where for many years she refused to consider returning to London or Windsor. She ordered that, in his memory, no changes were to be made to the house, and it remained very much in its original state until Victoria died there in 1901.

King Edward VII did not enjoy Osborne as much as he did Sandringham and he presented the house and most of its 1,000-acre estate to the nation in 1902, the year after his accession.

Today, Osborne House is part of English Heritage. The State Apartments, with their vast collection of priceless works of art, and part of the gardens, have been open to the public since 1904, but it wasn't until 1954 that the Queen gave permission for the private apartments to be opened. Part of the main property was converted into a Convalescent Home for Officers and is not open, but the Swiss Cottage in the grounds, built when the main house was bought, opens along with the rest of the estate.

# ℨ

## Abdication and Accession

Britain does not have a tradition of abdication, unlike, for example, the Netherlands, where, once the Sovereign has reached a certain age, he or she is expected to retire and make way for a younger Monarch.

In Britain, it is a job for life and, in fact, only one British Sovereign has ever abdicated, when King Edward VIII gave up the throne in December 1936 in order to marry the American, double divorcée, Mrs Wallis Warfield Simpson. The Prime Minister, Stanley Baldwin, announced the abdication in the House of Commons on 4 December 1936. The reasons given were that the Government would not accept Mrs Simpson as Queen because the Church of England did not recognise divorce or the remarriage of someone whose previous spouse was still living.

The Sovereign does not require the permission of the Government to marry, as the Royal Marriage Act 1772 does not apply to the Monarch (see Royal Marriages).

However, Government Ministers are allowed to offer advice informally to the Sovereign (if he is male) on whether they consider his bride-to-be to be a suitable queen. In the case of Edward and Mrs Simpson, the opposite view was formed and the King, who refused to give up the woman he loved, chose instead to relinquish the Throne and, for the rest of his life, was required to live outside the country he once ruled.

Although shock waves were felt throughout the country and the Empire, there were no constitutional issues caused by the abdication. The succession was seamless, with Prince Albert, Duke of York, Edward's brother, taking over immediately, becoming King George VI.

So, apart from this single instance, there has never been an abdication in Britain. Any suggestion that the Queen, now in her eighties, will abdicate in favour of her son, the Prince of Wales, is never going to be adopted. At her coronation, the Queen swore an oath to serve as Sovereign until she dies and that is what is going to happen. Indeed, many people believe that for the stability of the Monarchy to continue, it is to be hoped that Her Majesty has inherited the longevity genes of her mother, who lived until the age of 101. The Prince of Wales, who is married to a divorced woman, whose previous husband is still living, will then be a very elderly man if and when he inherits the throne.

## Accession

Elizabeth II had been Queen Regnant (ruling in her own right) for several hours before she knew of her changed status. As Princess Elizabeth, she and her husband, the Duke of Edinburgh, were on a visit to Kenya, and it was while they were sleeping that her father, King George VI, had died at Sandringham back in England. Because of the time difference, the news was received at Treetops, the house they were staying at in a remote part of the country, in the early hours of the morning. The Duke was woken up and he then relayed the information to his wife that she was now Queen. When she was asked by what name she wished to be known, she replied, 'By my own, of course, Elizabeth.'

The moment the King died, his successor assumed the title of Sovereign, hence the cry 'The King is dead, long live the King (or Queen)', so the Monarchy never dies and the Royal Standard is never lowered over the place where the Sovereign is present. This was partly the reason for the confusion and anger when no flag was seen to be flying at half-mast on the death of the late Diana, Princess of Wales (see Royal Funerals).

As the Queen acceded to the throne on 6 February, this is the day that her accession is commemorated each year with royal salutes being fired at noon. If 6 February falls on a Sunday, the gun salutes are postponed until noon on the following day.

A Proclamation Council is held in St James's Palace (not Buckingham Palace) to which every member of the Privy Council is summoned, as well as Peers from the House of Lords (but not Members of Parliament from the Commons), the Lord Mayor of London and other dignitaries from the Commonwealth. Once the Proclamation has been announced, the Sovereign takes the oath, which includes defending the security of the Church of Scotland – not the Church of England – which is surprising to some as the Sovereign is the supreme Governor of the Church of England, but not of the Church of Scotland. That declaration takes place some months later, at the State Opening of Parliament, when the Sovereign vows to maintain the established Protestant succession

At the present time, no Roman Catholic, or anyone married to a Roman Catholic, may succeed to the throne, and members of the Royal Family who have married Catholics have been required to forfeit their place in the Line of Succession.

## Act of Settlement 1701

It is considered that the main ingredient of the Act of Settlement is that no Roman Catholic, nor anyone married to a Roman Catholic, is permitted to become Sovereign.

However, this exclusion applies only to Roman Catholics; members of any other religion are not barred from succeeding to the throne, even though the Coronation Oath demands allegiance to the Church of England.

In recent times, the male member of the Royal Family nearest to the throne in the Line of Succession who was forced to relinquish his position was His Royal Highness Prince Michael of Kent, who at one time, before the birth of the Queen's younger children and their subsequent offspring, occupied fifth place in the Line of Succession. On his marriage to Princess Michael, an Austrian Roman Catholic, Prince Michael gave up his place but, in reality, it was merely a gesture as there was virtually no chance of him ever becoming King as he moved further and further down the line.

The full title of the Act of Settlement 1701 is: 'An Act for the further limitation of the Crown and better securing the rights and liberties of the subject'.

At the time, it was thought necessary in case Catholics, under the influence of the Pope, would seek the Crown and the Protestant subjects would therefore suffer. So the main purpose of the Act was, and remains, to secure the Protestant succession to the throne.

The sovereign must swear an oath to maintain the Church of England and the Protestant religion and, since the Treaty of Union 1701, this has been extended to include the Church of Scotland. A fundamental principle of the Act is that the Sovereign alone cannot declare war (in spite of the fact that all wars are declared in the Monarch's name). Her Majesty would have to seek the consent of Parliament before any act of aggression towards another country. In this way the Act of Settlement reinforces and strengthens the development in Britain of a constitutional monarchy.

## Advertising

The Lord Chamberlain's Office issues strict rules concerning the use for commercial purposes of any images of members of the Royal Family. This includes photographs, portraits, engravings and busts. The rules prohibit the use of such images for advertising purposes on certain specific items including stamps (though, of course, the Queen's face appears on postage stamps not only in the United Kingdom but also many Commonwealth countries), articles of dress and furniture fabrics and soft furnishings, including curtains. The only time images of the Royal Family are allowed to be used in advertising books, films, radio or television programmes is when they have been officially sanctioned by Buckingham Palace.

Of course, in all the royal shops at Buckingham Palace, Windsor Castle, the Palace of Holyroodhouse, Hampton Court Palace and Sandringham, postcards are sold showing nearly every member of the Royal Family in a variety of poses. Where permission has been granted for an advertisement to appear bearing an image of the Royal Family, it is on condition that no indication must be given to imply that the goods or any other article has either been purchased by a family member or that they are endorsing the product.

One exception to the advertising rule is the Queen's grand-daughter, Zara Phillips (see Zara), who is a World Champion equestrian and, as such, has accepted sponsorship from a number of prestigious companies and she is used to advertise their wares in many publication throughout the world. The money she receives is used to help pay the expenses for her string of competitive horses.

## Animals

Members of the Royal Family are frequently given unusual gifts of animals, particularly when they make overseas visits. Among those given to the Queen are tortoises, sloths, oncas, beavers and an elephant, while she was also offered – and accepted – on behalf of Prince Andrew, a gift of a baby crocodile, during a State Visit to The Gambia in 1961. Her Majesty's private secretary kept it in his tin bath until it could be brought back to Britain.

The Duke of Edinburgh once received two pygmy hippopotami and Princess Anne was given a three-month-old brown Syrian bear named Nikki, who was found a permanent home in Regent's Park Zoo.

## Air Raids

During the Second World War, Buckingham Palace was hit nine times by German bombs; the first time in September 1940 and the last in July 1944 (see section on Royal Residences, Buckingham Palace). The chapel was totally destroyed in one attack and has never been replaced. The Queen's Gallery now stands on the site of what was the chapel, which is why, since the war, most royal christenings have taken place in the Music Room of the Palace.

It was following the first air raid on the Palace that Queen Elizabeth made her famous remark: 'Now I can look the East End in the face.' She was, of course, referring to the fact that much of London's East End had been almost totally destroyed during the Blitz bombing.

## Armed Forces

The Queen is Commander-in-Chief of all the armed forces of the United Kingdom and it is in her name that wars and peace are declared. However, as a constitutional Monarch, she cannot take these decisions without the consent and approval of Parliament.

At Buckingham Palace, the Queen employs a Defence Services Secretary (see Defence Services Secretary) who briefs her on all matters concerning the forces.

During the Second World War, as Princess Elizabeth, she served for a period in 1945 as an officer in the Auxiliary Territorial Service (ATS) – her number, which she says she can always remember, was 230873 – working in transport. Her Majesty claims she can still change a carburettor on a three-ton lorry.

She was the first (and so far only) female member of the Royal Family to become a full-time, serving soldier. Other female members of the family have held honorary appointments in a number of regiments, Royal Navy units and Royal Air Force squadrons, but none has joined the forces full time.

The Duke of Edinburgh served as an officer in the Royal Navy from 1939–52, seeing active wartime service and taking part in a number of naval battles. He captained his own ship, *HMS Magpie*, and had reached the rank of Commander when he was forced into early retirement in 1952 on the accession of his wife as Elizabeth II. He retains an association with his old service and now holds the rank of Admiral of the Fleet.

The Prince of Wales served in the Royal Navy as part of his training for kingship and commanded his own ship, *HMS Bronington*.

Prince Andrew joined the Royal Navy in 1979 and trained as a helicopter pilot, seeing active service in the Falklands Campaign in 1982 serving on board *HMS Invincible*.

Prince Edward joined the Royal Marines in 1983 but failed to complete his initial course and was not commissioned.

The Duke of Kent was commissioned into the Royal Scots Greys in 1955 and remained in the Army for 21 years during which time he served in Britain, Cyprus and Hong Kong before retiring with the rank of Lieutenant Colonel in 1976. He was subsequently promoted to the honorary rank of Major-General in 1983.

His younger brother, Prince Michael of Kent, was commissioned in the 11th Hussars (Prince Albert's Own) and retired from full-time service in the Army in 1981 with the rank of Major.

For ranks and appointments held by the Queen and other members of the Royal Family, see Appendix.

# B

## Banks

The Queen and every member of the Royal Family hold bank accounts at Coutts & Co in The Strand, London. Since the reign of George IV (1820–30), every Sovereign has maintained an account with the bank. Her Majesty possesses one of Coutts' distinctive cheque books surmounted, in her case, with a crown. Other members of the family have coronets on their chequebooks. However, it is unusual these days for anyone to receive a personal cheque from the Queen as, in the days when she did write them herself, the recipients often declined to present them for payment, preferring to keep them as souvenirs, so Her Majesty's accounts (handled by the Keeper of the Privy Purse) were sometimes difficult to balance.

Coutts normally requires clients to be able to prove they have upwards of £500,000 in liquid assets or £2 million in property values; not too much of a problem presumably for Her Majesty, but Queen Elizabeth, the Queen Mother, was believed to have a £4 million overdraft, which was settled after her death in 2001.

The company, founded in 1692, is part of the private banking arm of National Westminster Bank which itself is now owned by the Royal Bank of Scotland. A regular sight in London is the brougham (a light, four-wheeled, horse-drawn carriage) from the Royal Mews that is used to carry correspondence between the Palace and Coutts on an almost daily basis.

## Birthdays and Places of Birth

Although many people believe the Royal Family has close Scottish ties, only one member in recent years was born in Scotland – Princess Margaret was born at Glamis Castle on 21 August 1930. Every other member of the current Royal Family, with the exception of the Duke of Edinburgh, was born in England.

Prince Andrew (19 February 1960) was the first child to be born to a reigning Sovereign at Buckingham Palace since the birth of Queen Victoria's youngest child, Princess Beatrice, on 14 April 1857. Prince Charles was also born at Buckingham Palace (14 November 1948) but his mother was then Princess Elizabeth, as she was when Princess Anne (15 August 1950) was born at Clarence House. The youngest of the Queen's children, Prince Edward (10 March 1964) was also born at Buckingham Palace. The full list of Royal birth dates and places is as follows:

### Royal Times, Dates and Places of Birth

|  | Time | Date | Place |
| --- | --- | --- | --- |
| The Queen | 2.40 | 21.04.26 | 17 Bruton St, London |
| The Duke of Edinburgh | Unknown | 10.06.21 | Mon Repos, Corfu |
| Prince of Wales | 21.14 | 14.11.48 | Buckingham Palace |
| Prince William | 21.03 | 21.06.82 | St Mary's Hospital |
| Prince Harry | 16.20 | 15.09.84 | St Mary's Hospital |
| Prince Andrew | 15.30 | 19.02.60 | Buckingham Palace |
| Princess Beatrice | 20.18 | 08.08.88 | Portland Hospital |
| Princess Eugenie | 19.58 | 23.03.90 | Portland Hospital |
| Prince Edward | 20.20 | 10.03.64 | Buckingham Palace |
| Viscount (James) Severn | 16.20 | 17.12.07 | Frimley Park Hospital |
| Lady Louise Windsor | Unknown | 08.11.03 | Frimley Park Hospital |
| Princess Anne | 11.50 | 15.08.50 | Clarence House |
| Peter Phillips | 10.46 | 15.11.77 | St Mary's Hospital |
| Zara Phillips | 20.15 | 15.08.81 | St Mary's Hospital |

The Queen is the only person in the country to have two birthdays: her actual birth date and her official one. The usual explanation given for the official birthday is that during the reign of King Edward VII, whose birthday was 9 November, he took part in the Trooping the Colour Parade (see Trooping the Colour), which is held to mark the occasion, and because of the inclement weather decided, for his own and his guests' welfare, to have another 'official' birthday in the summer months. Since 1959, The Queen's official birthday has been celebrated on a Saturday in June when the Parade is held on Horseguards, gun salutes are fired at noon and a flypast by aircraft of the RAF takes place along The Mall and over Buckingham Palace.

## Birthday Greetings

With longevity now extending well beyond the accepted life-span of three-score-years-and-ten, an increasing number of men and women now receive a message from the Queen congratulating them on reaching their 100th birthday. It is a practice that was started by Her Majesty's grandfather, King George V, in 1917. It used to be in the form of a telegram but, since they no longer exist, a more prosaic telemessage is now sent from Buckingham Palace. The nice thing about it is that recipients do not have to pay. It's entirely free as long as they can prove they are 100 and documentary proof is required to prevent fraud and hoax attempts.

### How to Apply for a 100th Birthday Greeting

Application is made to this address: The Anniversaries Office, Buckingham Palace, London SW1A 1AA.

Apply no later than three weeks before the birthday but, if you forget, it is possible to receive a belated congratulatory message up to six months after the event.

An application form is sent which has to be returned to the Palace, together with a birth certificate, but if no certificate can be found, then someone from the Pensions Service is asked to call to see the recipient to check on their credentials.

People who have moved to live abroad, or were born or married overseas, may still receive a message from the Queen as long as they provide photocopies of their passports.

Once the 100th birthday has been passed, a further message of congratulation is sent on the occasion of the 105th birthday and every year thereafter. The message normally consists of a photograph of the Queen with a personal greeting followed by Her Majesty's signature.

Of course, the most famous person ever to receive a greeting from the Queen was her mother, the late Queen Elizabeth, the Queen Mother, who celebrated her 100th birthday on 4 August 2000. The only difference between her card and all the others was that the Queen signed hers 'Lillibet', the pet name by which she was known to her mother and her sister, Princess Margaret.

## Books

Many authors dedicate their books to the Queen and send copies to Buckingham Palace personally inscribed. Before they are allowed to do so, the books are all delivered to the Ecclesiastical Household where they are read to ensure nothing 'unsuitable' is placed before royal eyes. This custom dates from medieval times when nearly all publications were religious and, as the Sovereign is Supreme Head of the Church of England, nothing that might be considered to be contrary to the Church ethics was allowed at Court. Even today, there is strict censorship of books and publications that are allowed to be given to the Queen and, if an author wishes to inscribe the book (which must always be hardback, never paperback), he or she is 'advised' of the correct form of wording: *'Dedicated to Her Majesty Queen Elizabeth II with respectful good wishes'* is felt to be perfectly acceptable in most cases.

The bookshops at Buckingham Palace, Windsor Castle (where there are two) and other royal residences stock a number of books about Royalty and among them are several bestsellers. Perennial favourites are books about the Royal Mews and the Royal Collection. The bookshops also sell postcards bearing photographs of the Royal Family, which are updated from time to time.

## Bridesmaids and Page Boys

Princess Elizabeth's bridesmaids at Westminster Abbey were: Princess Margaret; Princess Alexandra; Lady Caroline Montagu-Douglas-Scott; Lady Mary Cambridge; Lady Elizabeth Mary Lambart; the Hon Pamela Mountbatten; the Hon Margaret Elphinstone, the Hon Diana Bowes-Lyon.

The Page Boys were the Princess's two young cousins, Prince William of Gloucester and Prince Michael of Kent.

## Brushing Rooms

All of the Queen's and the Prince of Wales's residences have Brushing Rooms, where the uniforms of the male members of the family are kept in pristine condition.

At Buckingham Palace, Her Majesty maintained a special Brushing Room, dedicated to the memory of her father, containing every one of his dozens of uniforms – Army, Royal Navy and Royal Air Force – plus those lightweight versions, worn when he was overseas, and those of Commonwealth countries. The uniforms were complete with medal ribbons, shirts, ties, cuff-links, socks and shoes, all of which were brushed and pressed every week by a valet.

The Queen refused to allow the Brushing Room to be changed in any way during the lifetime of her mother, even when officials asked for the uniforms, many of which were unique, as the regiments and units they were associated with had disappeared years ago, to be displayed in an exhibition. It was eventually emptied shortly after the death of the Queen Mother in 2002.

The current Brushing Room at the Palace contains the naval uniforms of the Duke of Edinburgh and those belonging to the regiments of which he is Colonel-in-Chief.

The Princess Royal's uniforms are also kept at Buckingham Palace, where the one she is seen in most regularly is that of the Blues and Royals, of which she is Colonel-in-Chief, and which she wears, when mounted, on parade at the Trooping the Colour ceremony.

At Clarence House, the Brushing Room contains not only the scores of uniforms worn by the Prince of Wales, during and since his service in the Royal Navy and the RAF, but also those of Prince William and Prince Harry.

# C

## Cars

The Queen's cars are garaged in the Royal Mews (see Royal Mews) at Buckingham Palace unless they are required at one of the other Royal residences. The official cars include seven State limousines: five are Rolls-Royces and two are Daimlers. They are all painted in the distinctive royal maroon livery and the Rolls-Royces do not carry number plates.

The most impressive and recent of the State limousines is a magnificent Rolls-Royce Phantom costing £250,000 that was a gift to Her Majesty from the Society of Motor Manufacturers and Traders to mark her Golden Jubilee in 2002. They also presented a Phantom VI model in 1978 costing £60,000, at the time of her Silver Jubilee the previous year.

The State limousines, which are fully air-conditioned, have removable rear roof coverings, which expose a transparent Perspex inner dome that enables the Queen and the Duke of Edinburgh to be seen. During the hours of darkness, fluorescent tubes light the interior. The interior contains a clock and CD player but no cocktail cabinet. The rear seats are four inches higher than usual and the carpet and lambs' wool rugs are pale blue.

When the Queen is a passenger, her own private mascot is attached to the vehicle. Designed by Edward Seago, it takes the form of a naked St George mounted over a slain dragon and is transferred to whatever car Her Majesty is using.

The Queen is always driven by her chief chauffeur or his assistant and her personal protection officer (see Police) sits alongside the driver. It is the protection officer who opens the door for the Queen; the chauffeur always remains behind the wheel facing forward.

When being driven in London or the Home Counties privately, the Queen prefers to use a Daimler Jaguar saloon in dark green (it is called Edinburgh Green). Although the Queen holds a valid driving licence, she has never taken a driving test, but she is an enthusiastic motorist since she was 18 and was given a car by her father that bore the registration number JGY 280, a number she has retained for nostalgic reasons and has had transferred to many different cars.

Her Majesty no longer drives in London but she is often seen around Windsor, Balmoral and Sandringham at the wheel of a Vauxhall or Jaguar, when to the dismay of the motoring organisations she refuses to wear a seat belt.

## Changing of the Guard

The most frequent and regular royal ceremonial is the changing of the guard. It takes place every morning in the summer (as long as it is not too wet) and every other day in the winter.

### How to Change the Guard

The Old Guard forms up in Friary Court in St James's Palace, which visitors can see clearly from Marlborough Road, at 11.00am.

They march down The Mall to Buckingham Palace, entering through the left-hand gate.

Meanwhile, the New Guard has marched from its base at Wellington Barracks in Birdcage Walk, and with both guards on parade on the forecourt of the Palace, the regimental band plays for 30 minutes while the guards march and counter-march in slow time and the captain of the Old Guard hands over the keys of the Palace to his opposite number in the New Guard. It is a splendid sight and one that attracts thousands of tourists from all over the world.

## Christenings

Traditionally, christenings in the Royal Family have always been private services with only the family, Godparents (see Godparents) and some close friends invited. During the 20th century, only one member of the family, Princess Eugenie, daughter of the Duke and Duchess of York, has been christened with the public present. This took place on 23 December 1990 during morning service at the church of St Mary Magdalene at Sandringham by the Bishop of Norwich. This was because the Royal Family were already at Sandringham for the Christmas holidays, so it would have been pointless returning to Buckingham Palace.

When the Queen, as Princess Elizabeth, was christened on 29 May 1926, there was still a private chapel at Buckingham Palace and that is where the ceremony took place under the guidance of the Archbishop of York, Dr Cosmo Gordon Lang. By the time Prince Charles, Princess Anne and Prince Andrew were to be christened, the chapel had disappeared and the Music Room inside the Palace was used for christening services.

Prince Charles – 15 December 1948, Buckingham Palace, christened by the Archbishop of Canterbury, Dr Geoffrey Fisher (who subsequently carried out the Coronation)

Princess Anne – 21 October 1950, Buckingham Palace, christened by the Archbishop of York, Dr Cyril Forster Garbett

Prince Andrew – 8 April 1960, Buckingham Palace, christened by the Archbishop of Canterbury, Dr Geoffrey Fisher

Prince Edward – 2 May 1964, Windsor Castle (Private Chapel), christened by the Dean of Windsor, Robert Woods

Peter Phillips (son of the Princess Royal) – 22 December 1977, Buckingham Palace, christened by the Archbishop of Canterbury, Dr Donald Coggan

Prince William of Wales – 4 August 1982, St George's Chapel, Windsor

Prince Henry (Harry) of Wales – 21 December 1984, St George's Chapel, Windsor, christened by Dr Robert Runcie, Archbishop of Canterbury

Zara Phillips (the Princess Royal's daughter) – 27 July 1981, Private Chapel, Windsor, Christened by the Dean of Windsor, the Rt Rev Michael Mann

Princess Beatrice (elder daughter of the Duke of York) – 20 December 1988, the Chapel Royal, St James's Palace, christened by the Archbishop of York

Princess Eugenie (younger daughter of the Duke of York) – 23 December 1990, the church of St Mary Magdalene, Sandringham, christened by the Bishop of Norwich

Lady Louise Windsor (daughter of the Earl and Countess of Wessex) – 24 April 2004, the Private Chapel, Windsor Castle

James Viscount Severn (son of the Earl and Countess of Wessex) – 21 April 2008, the Private Chapel, Windsor Castle

## Christening Robe

Every royal baby since 1841, when Queen Victoria's eldest daughter Victoria, the Princess Royal, first wore it, has worn the same christening robe made of Honiton lace, lined with white satin. The robe is beautifully preserved in pristine condition and is brought out at regular intervals to make sure no damage has occurred in the nearly two centuries since it was first used. The Queen and her sister, Princess Margaret, both wore it, as did all their children and grandchildren, as well as the Queen's father and his siblings and her grandfather and great-grandfather – and their children and grandchildren.

The longevity of the garment is testimony to the skill of the original seamstress and also to the loving care that has been bestowed on it since Queen Victoria's days. The original robe has now been placed in a special container to preserve it and for the christenings of the Earl of Wessex's children, Lady Louise Windsor and Viscount Severn, Angela Kelly, the Queen's senior dresser and personal assistant and her team, made an exact replica that is impossible to distinguish from the original.


## Christmas – Cards, Coal and Church

The Queen and Prince Philip send around 850 Christmas cards to Heads of State, leading politicians, Commonwealth leaders, friends and family. But Her Majesty and His Royal Highness do not sit down and sign them together. The Queen used to sign hers on board the Royal Yacht during the summer cruise. But since Britannia has been decommissioned, she adds her signature while she is at Balmoral, and then they are passed to Philip for him to sign. He also sends a further 200 on his own, to the military, naval and civilian organisations with which he is associated.

Recipients can tell their standing with the Queen by the way in which their cards are inscribed. Cousins like the Gloucesters and Kents have theirs signed 'Lillibet' – the Queen's childhood nickname – while political figures such as the Prime Minister, Lord Chancellor and the Speaker of the House of Commons get a formal 'Elizabeth R' and 'Philip'. Close friends like Countess Mountbatten will receive a card bearing the legend 'Elizabeth' and 'Philip' (hand-written) without the 'R' (Regina) and those who just make it on to the Christmas card list, including former senior members of the Royal Household; usually find theirs isn't even personally signed. The signature is simply stamped on.

The Queen also gives around 1,450 Christmas puddings to all her staff, pensioners, the men and women who work in the Court Post Office, 50 or so of the men from the Department of the Environment who look after the fabric of the building and the Palace police force. The puddings used to come from Harrods, but in recent years, the Keeper of the Privy Purse had invited tenders from different firms – and it is usually the cheapest one that wins!

By tradition the Queen gives one hundredweight of coal to 'deserving and needy' people living in Windsor. In the early days of her reign, these numbered around 900; today the figure is less than 100 as central heating has, in the main, done away with the need for coal fires.

Staff in the Royal Household are given their presents from the Queen during the week before she leaves for the holiday. They line up in strict order of seniority with Members first, followed by Officials, with Staff bringing up the rear. That evening they are also invited to the Household Christmas reception that is held in the State Apartments at Buckingham Palace.

In the days before Christmas, those family members who have been invited to spend the holiday with the Queen and Prince Philip are told in what order they are to arrive at Sandringham and at what time. Royal protocol being what it is, it's all worked out in accordance with precedence and seniority, the most junior and least important arriving first with Prince Charles, the Duchess of Cornwall, Prince William and Prince Harry always being the last to turn up.

The Queen likes to put the finishing touches to decorating the tree herself, helped by some of the younger members of the family. The tree comes from her estate and she also gives trees to several churches.

## Christmas Trees Gifted by the Queen

Westminster Abbey – two trees
St Paul's Cathedral – three trees
The Guards Chapel, Wellington Barracks – two trees
St Giles Cathedral, Edinburgh – one tree
Canongate Kirk, Edinburgh – one tree
Crathie Church, Balmoral – one tree
Churches and schools near Sandringham also receive trees
from the Queen

Royal Christmas presents are traditionally exchanged at teatime on Christmas Eve, not on Christmas morning like everyone else. This is because, unlike most people today, the Queen still regards Christmas as a religious festival, so she likes to reserve Christmas morning for church. Trestle tables are laid out in the Red Drawing Room with sections marked off with tape showing where each family member's gifts should be.

During the afternoon, they all creep down to the drawing room and secretly place their gifts on the table. The rule is that no one may open their parcel until given permission by Prince Philip who supervises the proceedings and also every present should be an inexpensive 'joke gift' – the cheaper the better. After all, what else can you give the family that has everything?

All the family attend church at Sandringham on Christmas morning but the Queen receives Holy Communion privately from her own chaplain before the service (see Religion). And when the collection plate is passed around, Her Majesty's equerry, who sits in the pew immediately behind her, hands her a brand new ten-pound note. It used to be a fiver, but inflation has caught up with them, as with the rest of us

As in most households, lunch is the main meal of the day, but there are five lunches served at Sandringham on Christmas Day. First the junior staff have theirs at 11.00am, then the senior footmen an hour later, followed by the Royal Family at 1.15pm. The junior kitchen staff have theirs at 2.15pm before everything comes to a halt so that they can all watch the Queen's Christmas broadcast at 3.00pm. Senior footmen and butlers sit down next and the royal chef is the last to have his lunch at around 4.00pm.

After dinner on Christmas evening, which is very formal, with the men in black tie and the ladies in long evening gowns and diamond tiaras, the family plays charades until midnight and nobody is permitted to go to bed until the Queen retires. Boxing Day is devoted to a large shooting party organised by the Duke of Edinburgh, after which everyone but the immediate family leaves Sandringham.

The Queen stays on until the beginning of February and – as she is not in the least bit superstitious – she insists on the Christmas decorations remaining up until she leaves. Taking them down, as most people do, on Twelfth Night, does not apply when you are royal.

## Civil List

The Civil List is the amount of money allocated by Parliament to enable the Monarchy to meet its public expenses. It was in 1689 that the House of Commons decided that, contrary to previous arrangements, whereby the Sovereign paid for both public defence and the Royal Household out of the hereditary revenues received by the Monarch, and therefore had total control, Parliament itself would decide how much would be paid to the Sovereign and it would retain the power to pay for the armed forces.

The first Civil List amounted to £1.2 million, of which half went to the King and half for public defence. It was in 1760 that the biggest change was made to the allowances paid to the Sovereign when it was agreed that in exchange for the Sovereign surrendering all his revenues, except those from the Duchy of Lancaster and the Duchy of Cornwall, Parliament would make an arrangement to pay what is now known as the Civil List for the duration of each reign.

It has only been in the present reign that the Civil List has been set for ten years with provision for an increase in line with inflation. It has been worked out that under the present system, with the Queen agreeing to surrender her rights to hereditary revenues, the country actually makes a profit out of the Monarchy, for if she had retained her rights, she would be receiving far more than the amount she gets under the Civil List. No money from the Civil List goes towards the Queen's personal expenditure; that all comes from the Duchy of Lancaster (see Duchy of Lancaster).

## The College of Arms

The College of Arms, the ultimate authority in England, Wales, Northern Ireland and the Commonwealth on all matters relating to heraldry and coats of arms, was established in 1484 by Richard III, with the present charter being granted by Mary Tudor in 1555.

The College, in Queen Victoria Street, opposite the City of London School, houses all the records of grants of arms in the above countries, and also holds records in respect of family pedigrees. Its library is the largest of its kind in the world, with its extensive collection of heraldic and genealogical material. Members of the public from all over the world visit or contact the College, seeking details of family trees and to find out if they may display armorial bearings. Newly appointed peers are advised on the design for their coats of arms.

The present establishment of the College of Arms consists of three Kings of Arms (Garter, Clarenceux and Norroy and Ulster), six Heralds (Lancaster, Somerset, Chester, Richmond, Windsor, York), and four pursuivants (Bluemantle, Portcullis, Rouge Croix, Rouge Dragon), whose seniority is decided by the date of their appointment.

Garter King of Arms is the most senior, who is appointed by the Queen on the advice of the Earl Marshal, the Duke of Norfolk, Premier Duke of England. It is a full-time paid post with the bulk of his income derived from his own private Heraldic and Genealogical practice. In addition, he receives small honoraria from the Home Office and the Ministry of Defence for 'State business'.

One of Garter's privileges is access to the Queen, through her private secretary.

In addition, there are five Heralds Extraordinary and one Pursuivant Extraordinary – New Zealand, Maltravers, Norfolk, Wales, Arundel, Fitzalan. Although not members of the corporation, they are appointed by Warrant under the Queen's Sign Manual and advise Garter and the College in certain specialist areas, e.g. the Law, Military Heraldry, Public Relations, Honours and Awards, State Ceremonial, etc. Like their full time colleagues, they have a ceremonial role and take part in the Annual Garter Service and the State Opening of Parliament, wearing tabards that bear the arms of the constituent countries of the United Kingdom.

There are no female Heralds or Pursuivants and there has never been a woman Garter King of Arms.

Much of the day-to-day work is centred around heraldic and genealogical research by the Heralds for their clients, who pay a fee depending on the amount of work involved. Coats of Arms continue to be granted by letters patent from the King of Arms.

Scotland has its own authority on such matters, known as Lord Lyon King of Arms, who has his headquarters in Lyon Court in Edinburgh.

## Confirmations

All members of the Royal Family have been confirmed into the Church of England. The Archbishop of Canterbury, Cosmo Gordon Lang, confirmed the Queen, as Princess Elizabeth, on 28 March 1940, shortly before her 16th birthday in the Private Chapel, Windsor Castle.

Both Prince Charles and Princess Anne were also confirmed in the Private Chapel, Charles on 13 April 1965 and Anne on 5 April 1966, with the Archbishop of Canterbury, Dr Michael Ramsey, officiating.

By the time of the confirmations of Her Majesty's two youngest children, the service had been transferred to St George's Chapel at Windsor Castle. Dr Donald Coggan was Archbishop of Canterbury when Andrew was confirmed on 13 April 1976, followed by Edward on 5 April 1978.

## Coronation Robes and Dresses

The Robes worn by the Queen at her coronation on 2 June 1953 had previously been worn by several of her ancestors, including her father in 1937, her grandfather, George V, in 1911, and even as far back as King George IV in 1821. The robes comprise a supertunica, mantle and stole and it is only the stole that was made especially for the Queen. It was a gift from some of the Commonwealth countries that acknowledged her as their Queen and the decoration includes symbols from Ceylon (now Sri Lanka), New Zealand, India, Australia and Canada, as well as St Edwards' Crown, the crossed keys of St Peter, the imperial eagle, the shamrock of Ireland, the leek of Wales, the Tudor rose and the thistle of Scotland, plus the flags of St Patrick, St Andrew and St George. As the base of the stole is gold in colour, the leek of Wales was chosen because the customary daffodil would not show up sufficiently against it.

Together, the supertunica and the Imperial Mantle, representing the four corners of the earth, weigh 23 pounds, so were a considerable burden for the slim 26-year-old Queen to carry throughout the ceremony.

The dress that the Queen wore under the tunic was chosen by her from a selection of designs and materials submitted by Norman Hartnell. It was made of cream satin and embroidered with the four symbols of the home nations – England, Ireland, Scotland and Wales – with Mr Hartnell insisting that for Wales the daffodil should be used. He was overruled by the powers that be at the Welsh Office, who demanded that the national emblem of Wales should be the leek, only for Hartnell to shout, 'I don't want an onion on one of my dresses.' But the bureaucrats won out and the leek replaced the daffodil.

## Counsellors of State

Counsellors of State are appointed to carry out, on a temporary basis, some of the Sovereign's duties when the Queen is absent. They are appointed from within the Royal Family from the Duke of Edinburgh and the four adults next in the line of succession.

### Current Counsellors of State

The Duke of Edinburgh, the Prince of Wales, Prince William, Prince Henry and the Duke of York.
On reaching their 21st birthdays, Princes William and Harry replaced the Earl of Wessex and the Princess Royal.

## Court Circular

Every morning, the *Times*, *Daily Telegraph*, *Independent* and the *Scotsman* contain a brief report on the previous day's activities of the Royal Family in what is known as The Court Circular.

The Circular is prepared in the Private Secretary's Office by the Information and Correspondence Section and has to be approved by the Queen before being released to the newspapers. The practice began with the appointment of a Court Newsman by King George

III, who became so annoyed at the inaccurate reporting of his activities that he ordered the papers to print his official version with not a single word changed or omitted.

In Queen Victoria's reign, the Court Newsman was required to attend personally at Buckingham Palace every day, including Sunday morning and afternoon. Before any official function – State Banquet, concert, reception or soirée – he was summoned to the Palace several days beforehand to copy out in longhand the names of every person on the guest list. His salary for this amounted to £45 a year, but obviously someone at the Palace felt that even this was excessive and, in 1909, it was reduced to £20. But it wasn't as bad as it seems, because then, as now, an astute editor would pay for information about Royalty, and social climbers would gladly slip the Court Newsman the odd guinea or two if he would insert their name in the Court Circular as near the Sovereign's as possible.

The position must have been highly sought after because Palace records show that from the first appointment to the last, when the post was abolished to make way for the first Press Secretary in 1918, nepotism was alive and well in this department with every Court Newsman passing the job on to his son or grandson.

# 𝔇

## Defence Services Secretary

The Defence Services Secretary is a serving officer in the armed forces, in the rank of Major General, Rear Admiral or Air Vice-Marshal, who is seconded to the Royal Household for three years in order to act as liaison between the Queen, the Ministry of Defence and the Chiefs of Staff. He maintains offices at Buckingham Palace, where most of his duties lie, and the Ministry of Defence in Whitehall.

At Buckingham Palace, the Defence Services Secretary works through the Private Secretary to the Queen for all matters concerning Her Majesty's relationship with the armed forces, apart from the Household Division, which has a separate connection with the Palace, and also No. 32 (the Royal) Squadron of the RAF, which has now assumed flying responsibilities for Her Majesty, in conjunction with the Director of Royal Travel, a former distinguished fighter pilot in the RAF, who is based at Buckingham Palace.

The Defence Services Secretary arranges, through the private secretary, any service invitations to the Sovereign, attendance on the Queen and other members of the Royal Family during service visits and arrangements for royal appointments within the services. If a regiment or other military or naval unit, or RAF squadron or station wants to invite a member of the Royal Family to accept an honorary appointment, the Defence Services Secretary acts as the link between the unit and the Palace.

## Defender of the Faith

It may seem surprising to find that the Queen, as Supreme Governor of the Church of England, carries a Roman Catholic title that was originally bestowed on her ancestor, Henry VIII, in 1521 by Pope Leo X.

An Act of Parliament in 1543 settled the title on The King and his successors in perpetuity, but it was Elizabeth I who first took the title Supreme Governor and, in 1570, issued a statement that she did not 'assume the use of any function or office of any ecclesiastical person', making clear her intention not to intrude on the spiritual ministry of the clergy.

Successive sovereigns have adhered to this rule and the Queen, in her role as Supreme Governor, has every five years since 1970, formally opened each newly elected General Synod of the Church of England.

The Prince of Wales caused something of a stir when he said in an interview that he would like to be considered defender of all faiths, not just that of the Church of England. It was an attempt to adjust to multi-culturalism and the many faiths now practised in the United Kingdom, but church leaders are thought to oppose any change in the Coronation Oath, or the title held by the Sovereign.

## Diamond Weddings

Every married couple in Britain and the Commonwealth who are celebrating a Diamond Wedding Anniversary (60 years) is eligible for a congratulatory message from the Queen. Since the Post Office stopped its Telegram Service in 1982, they are now delivered by post as a telemessage. The card contains, on the outside, the Royal Coat of Arms, with a drawing inside of one of four Royal residences – Windsor Castle, Caernarvon Castle, the Palace of Holyroodhouse or Killyleagh – depending on whether the recipient lives in England, Wales, Scotland or Northern Ireland. Anniversaries after the 60th receive congratulations every five years and, once the 70th has been reached, it is every year

In order to receive the messages, a friend or family member should notify the Queen's Assistant Private Secretary, Buckingham Palace, London SW1A 1AA, in plenty of time with proof of the occasion.

## Dine and Sleep

One of the most intriguing invitations it is possible to receive from the Queen is to be asked to 'dine and sleep' at Windsor Castle. During April, when the Court moves to Windsor, Her Majesty likes to invite around a dozen guests, with their spouses (but not partners of the same sex), to join her and Prince Philip for an evening that includes dinner, bed and breakfast. There is usually an eclectic gathering of politicians, businessmen, sports stars, church leaders and a sprinkling of people who are resident in the Castle. The invitation asks guests to arrive in the early evening, when a maid and valet are assigned to them for the duration of their visit. Their overnight bags are unpacked and, if necessary, clothes are pressed and sponged. They meet their royal hostess for drinks and then join her and His Royal Highness for dinner, after which the Queen conducts them to the Royal Library where a special exhibition has been arranged with the various guests' particular interests in mind. For example, if one of them is a literary figure, they might be shown a first edition of a Charles Dickens novel. The Queen goes to enormous lengths to choose the right subjects and guests rarely find there isn't something to interest them.

At the end of the evening, the Queen and Prince Philip bid farewell to the guests; they won't see them again during the visit. The guests leave after breakfast the next morning, with their bags carefully packed by their temporary servants.

## Tipping the Royal Domestic Staff

Overnight guests at any Royal residence find a note from the Master of the Household asking them not to leave tips for the staff, saying it is neither expected nor allowed.

However, most visitors do like to show their appreciation in a positive fashion and notes do change hands more often than not, especially after a weekend visit or a shooting party.

Stories abound among staff of ridiculously generous tips, usually offered by wealthy overseas visitors. One middle-eastern potentate, on alighting from his limousine, handed the footman a small, suede bag containing thousands of pounds' worth of diamonds. That was a gratuity that definitely had to be divided among his colleagues.

## Diplomatic Corps

All foreign emissaries to London are accredited to the Court of St James's (not Buckingham Palace). At the time of writing, there are 108 Embassies and 46 High Commissions (from the Commonwealth), of which some 4 High Commissions and 21 Embassies are non-resident. Each one has the right of direct communication with the Sovereign through the Marshal of the Diplomatic Corps, a retired senior officer, who serves in the Royal Household for ten years, from his office in Ambassador's Court, St James's Palace.

The Marshal arranges for the incoming and outgoing Ambassadors and High Commissioners to be received by the Queen and also for them to be invited to the State Opening of Parliament, Royal Ascot, Garden Parties and the most prestigious of all Royal social functions, The Diplomatic Reception. This is held at Buckingham Palace in November, with 1,000 guests including prominent British figures such as past Prime Ministers, the Archbishops of Canterbury and York, and members of the Cabinet, all wearing, as one guest described it, 'every rock in the book'.

The missions are placed throughout the State apartments, which are filled with the diplomatic and political élite of the nation, in order of precedence (this is not how large or important the country is, but the length of time the representative has been in office) and each Ambassador and High Commissioner is presented to the Queen and the Duke of Edinburgh. The royal couple methodically work the room, as polished and poised as any experienced politician running for office, after which there is a dance and a buffet supper is served.

## Dogs

Whenever the Queen is seen walking in the grounds of any of her homes, she is invariably accompanied by several of her dogs. Animals feature strongly in the lives of all the Royal Family but even though Corgi is the breed usually associated with the Queen, as she has these near her during the working week at Buckingham Palace, her own preference is said to be for working gun-dogs.

She breeds prize-winning black Labradors in the kennels at Sandringham, from where they are sold all over the world to enthusiasts for hundreds of pounds each. The Queen is a highly skilled handler in gun-dog trials but, because of security concerns, has been able to take part only in private events on her own land. However, on occasions, she has acted as a judge at Kennel Club Retriever Trials.

The kennels at Sandringham are among the finest in the country and the Queen takes a keen personal interest, naming all the puppies herself, with their official names being registered at the Kennel Club, all with the prefix 'Sandringham'.

## The Royal Corgis

The Corgis first arrived in the 1930s when the then Princess Elizabeth, and later her sister, Princess Margaret, were each given one by their parents.

The Queen has had many Corgis since then and they live in some splendour in the corridor immediately outside Her Majesty's sitting room in the Palace.

She keeps up to seven Corgis and they are very much her dogs and no one else's.

Visitors who attempt to get into her good books by patting the dogs are sharply told, 'Don't do that, they don't like it.' What she really means is she doesn't like it!

The Queen feeds the dogs from food prepared in the royal kitchens, where the proud boast is that they have never eaten anything from cans.

Each Corgi has its own feeding bowl and, once the footman has brought up the food and measured each meal, they wait until given the go-ahead from their royal mistress.

The Queen loves to look after their welfare personally, and she has even attended them when one has had an accident, cutting his foot, using some of her own homeopathic medicines. She was once overheard to remark, 'If it's good enough for me, it should be good enough for them.'

The Household do not regard the Corgis with the same affection as the Queen feels. The dogs have a habit of 'cocking their legs' wherever they feel like, and so the staff carry a supply of soda water and blotting paper, which is apparently the best way of dealing with any 'little' accidents.

## Dressers

The three people closest to the Queen in the domestic household are her dressers. They see her first thing in the morning, several times during the day and one of them is always on hand last thing at night. The ladies are supervised by Miss Angela Kelly, who has been so successful at guiding her royal mistress through the labyrinth of fashion that she has been promoted to the unique position of 'Personal Assistant, Advisor and Curator to Her Majesty the Queen (the Queen's Jewellery, Insignia and Wardrobe)'.

Miss Kelly, a vivacious and attractive woman, has been credited with almost single-handedly propelling the Queen into the 21st century with her style. Commentators have observed how, in recent years, Her Majesty's outfits have improved beyond measure, after decades of her being seen wearing the same old styles. For her efforts, Angela Kelly has been rewarded by being made a Member of the Royal Victorian Order, the Queen's personal Order of Chivalry. She has also been given her own office with a secretary attached and, although technically she is lower down the pecking order than many of the private secretaries and other Household luminaries, they all know that they offend her at their peril. She has the ear of the Queen in a way enjoyed by nobody else – even the Lord Chamberlain.

One of the dressers accompanies the Queen on her overseas visits to supervise the packing, ironing and laying-out of Her Majesty's outfits. The dressers receive a copy of the following day's programme the evening before, as they do in Britain, so they know exactly what to prepare, knowing that the Queen can change outfits up to five times in a single day. The Queen relies on her dressers to guide her discreetly in her choice of clothes and they know that they should not offer a selection – that is what they are paid to do. But if they get it wrong, royal disapproval is swift and final.

## Driving Licences

As part of the Royal Prerogative, Her Majesty does not have to possess a driving licence (the only person in the country with this unique exemption). Every other member of the Royal Family is required to pass the standard driving test and to hold a licence if they wish to drive on public roads. The Queen's four children were all given lessons by their mother, father and chauffeurs from the Royal Mews on the private roads at Windsor and Sandringham. Both Prince Charles and Princess Anne also took extra lessons at the Metropolitan Police Driving School before taking their tests, passing first time.

The Prince of Wales passed on 11 April 1967.

Princess Anne passed in 1968; she is the only one of the Queen's children to hold a Heavy Goods Vehicle (HGV) Licence, taking the test so she could drive her horsebox to venues when she was competing in Three-Day Events.

Prince Andrew passed at Isleworth on 21 December 1977.

Prince Edward passed at Wanstead on 27 July 1981.

## Duchy of Cornwall

The Prince of Wales does not receive any money or allowances from the State or from the Queen. His income, which in 2009 amounted to a little over £14 million, comes from the Duchy of Cornwall, a royal estate created in 1337 by Edward III for his eldest son, Edward, the Black Prince, and all subsequent eldest sons of the Sovereign have benefited from this highly profitable organisation.

Prince Charles, who also bears the title Duke of Cornwall (see Titles), has received his income from the Duchy of Cornwall since he was just six years old, when his mother came to the Throne in 1952.

The Duchy Estate consists of approximately 54,424 hectares in 23 counties, mainly in the south-west of England, including the Scilly Isles. The single most valuable area though is 45 acres of prime property in the Kennington area of London and Prince Charles, or the Duchy, is landlord of the famous Oval cricket ground. However, just because Charles is the beneficiary of the Duchy, he is not allowed to sell any part of it on a personal whim; he is only entitled to its annual income on which he pays income tax.

Her Majesty's Treasury oversees the finances of the estate and the Duchy has to have the approval and consent of the Treasury for all property transactions of more than £500,000. The annual accounts are laid before both Houses of Parliament so that the Treasury can be seen to fulfil its statutory responsibilities.

The board of the Duchy meets twice a year, chaired by the Prince of Wales, who plays an active part in every aspect of the estate's functions. The Duchy funds the public, charitable and private functions of The Prince of Wales, Prince William and Prince Harry, as well as those of the Duchess of Cornwall.

The headquarters of the Duchy is based in an office in Buckingham Gate where its full-time administrator devotes his time to the worldly concerns of making money – lots of it. When Prince Charles accedes to the Throne, his elder son William will become both Prince of Wales and Duke of Cornwall and he will then take over the running of the Duchy – and receive its income.

One little known side benefit that is also enjoyed by the Duke of Cornwall is that if anyone dies intestate within the Duchy and no one is legally able to claim the estate, it then belongs to the Duchy of Cornwall. The present Duke has always insisted that any money or property obtained in this manner should be donated to charity.

## Duchy of Lancaster

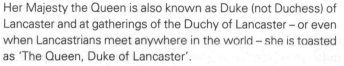

Her Majesty the Queen is also known as Duke (not Duchess) of Lancaster and at gatherings of the Duchy of Lancaster – or even when Lancastrians meet anywhere in the world – she is toasted as 'The Queen, Duke of Lancaster'.

This somewhat unusual state of affairs has its origins in 1267 when Henry III created his second son, Edmund, Duke of Lancaster. Since then, every British sovereign has retained the title Duke of Lancaster to ensure that there was a separation between this inheritance and any other possession held by the Crown.

The estate revenues, as with the Duchy of Cornwall, exist to provide a private income for the holder of the title, in this case, the Duke of Lancaster.

By virtue of various means, including fortuitous marriages, seizure and astute buying, the estate now totals over 50,000 acres of mainly agricultural land in Lancashire, Yorkshire, Staffordshire, Shropshire, Cheshire, Northamptonshire, Lincolnshire and Glamorganshire in South Wales.

But by far the most important and valuable holdings are in the centre of London where freeholds are owned in The Strand and Regent Street and the Queen, through the Duchy, also owns the land on which the Savoy Hotel stands. This came about in 1284 when Queen Eleanor gave her son Edmund the Manor of the Savoy.

The Duchy is administered by a Chancellor, an office held by a member of the Government and appointed by the Prime Minister with the approval of the Sovereign. The office dates from 1363 and today a Council and a permanent staff of professional land administrators advise the Chancellor. Nowadays, the County Palatine comprises the modern administrative counties of Lancashire, Greater Manchester, Merseyside and Furness in Cumbria, and the Duchy of Lancaster continues to exercise functions such as the appointment of High Sheriffs.

The Duchy office administers the estate of any person dying intestate within the Palatine County and Her Majesty, as Duke of Lancaster, also has the right to make appointments to 42 church livings in this area. One final responsibility of the Duchy is the administration and expenses of the Queen's Chapel of the Savoy, the Chapel of the Royal Victorian Order.

## Ecclesiastical Household

One of the highest honours for any clergyman is to be appointed to the Ecclesiastical Household of the Queen. There are three forms of chaplain in the Household: Chaplains to the Queen, Domestic Chaplains and Chaplains of the Chapel Royal.

The Chaplains to the Queen, who belong to the College of Chaplains, are selected from all dioceses and their duties include preaching at the Chapel Royal, St James's Palace or The Queen's Chapel, St James's Palace, according to the Rota of Waits (or list of preachers). There are around 40 chaplains at any one time, under the supervision of the Clerk of the Closet, who is a Bishop, and they normally retire at 70.

Domestic chaplains serve in the private chapels at Buckingham Palace (where services are held for members of the Royal Household) and Windsor Castle. The Rector of St Mary Magdalene, Sandringham, and the Minister of Crathie Parish Church near Balmoral, are appointed as extra domestic chaplains.

The third category is the Chaplains of the Chapels Royal, who work under the Bishop of London in the Chapels Royal at St James's Palace, Hampton Court Palace and the Tower of London.

All members of the Ecclesiastical Household wear scarlet cassocks with the former chaplains wearing either a silver gilt chaplain badge or a silver priest's badge.

Scotland has its own Ecclesiastical Household headed by the Dean of the Chapel Royal in Scotland assisted by ten chaplains to the Queen.

Four padres in each of the armed services are appointed as Honorary Chaplains to the Queen and they, too, are entitled to wear the scarlet cassock.

There are no Roman Catholic Chaplains to the Queen, or clergy of any religion other than Protestant.

## Engagements

The Queen's public engagements are arranged up to two years in advance, particularly when an overseas visit is being planned. However, there are certain fixed 'feasts' in her domestic calendar that have to be included every year without fail.

A Selection of Royal Engagements

The Royal Maundy Service on the Thursday before Easter Sunday
The Garter Service on the Monday of the Royal Ascot Meeting
The Summer Royal Ascot Meeting
The Sovereign's Birthday Parade (Trooping the Colour)
The Court's move to the Palace of Holyroodhouse for one week in July
The Royal British Legion Annual Festival of Remembrance in the Royal Albert Hall
The Cenotaph ceremony in Whitehall on Remembrance Sunday in November
*All the above ceremonies are excellent opportunities for the public to see the Queen and the Royal Family at comparatively close quarters.*

Her Majesty also reacts spontaneously to major disasters in the United Kingdom with personal visits to the sites of such calamities as the Lockerbie Bombing and the Aberfan tip collapse – once she has been assured that she will not be in the way.

## Equerries

There are several different types of equerry (the accent is on the second syllable). However, the one most often seen is the young service officer attached to the Queen and almost invariably in uniform. When the Prime Minister makes his official visit to Her Majesty every Tuesday evening, he is introduced into the royal presence by her equerry. The title comes from the French word '*écurie*' meaning stable, and originally they worked in the Royal Mews managing horses for the sovereign.

The Crown Equerry today is still the man responsible for running the Royal Mews, but the equerry attached to the Queen for three years has nothing to do with horses. He is selected from each of the armed forces in turn and a term at Buckingham Palace is said to do his service career no harm whatsoever.

Arguably the man who gained the greatest benefit from being an equerry is Vice-Admiral Tim Laurence, who not only met the Princess Royal during his term of office, he also married her.

There is also a senior and permanent equerry who is Deputy Master of the Household and whose duties are confined to organising the Royal Family's domestic arrangements.

Apart from the Queen, others members of the Royal Family appoint equerries from time to time: the Duke of Edinburgh has one service equerry and two temporary equerries; the Prince of Wales and the Duke of York have a service equerry each; and all the members of the Royal Family select their equerries from among the regiments, naval units and RAF squadrons with which they are associated, including those from Commonwealth countries, particularly if they are about to visit that country as local knowledge is invaluable during an official visit.

## Eton College

The most famous school in the world, Eton College, (known to locals disdainfully as 'Slough Grammar') was founded by Henry VI in 1440. Its full name is The Royal College of Our Lady at Eton by Windsor and its location, just across the river from Windsor Castle, has meant a continuous connection with Royalty.

Queen Victoria and Prince Albert were frequent visitors and, in more recent times, both Prince William and Prince Harry were pupils at the school. Prince William used to spend part of his Sunday afternoons visiting his grandmother, the Queen, to have tea and also to be schooled in some of the issues with which he will need to be familiar when he becomes King.

The College has a reputation for excellence and generations of former pupils have gone on to become high-ranking servants of the Crown, as well as many Prime Ministers, archbishops and senior officers in the Army and Royal Navy.

One tradition that is jealously guarded by the school is that, since the death of Queen Victoria, the boys have always formed part of the Guard of Honour within the grounds of Windsor Castle at all Royal funerals.

## Fabergé

The Royal Family, Fabergé Collection is said to be among the most important of its kind in the world. Carl Fabergé, goldsmith to the Imperial Russian Royal Family, recognised this when he opened his London branch in 1903 with his main clients being King Edward VII and Queen Alexandra. Since then, successive Monarchs and their wives have added to the collection, including the fabulous Mosaic Egg of 1914, that was bought by Queen Mary in 1934, which, when opened, reveals the entire family of Czar Nicholas II, while the Queen's father, King George VI, bought many examples of Fabergé's magnificent cigarette cases. There are also some 300 animals carved in semi-precious stones.

The Queen and her mother, the late Queen Elizabeth, the Queen Mother, also purchased a number of Fabergé items, many of which have been displayed at special exhibitions in The Queen's Gallery, though the collection is normally housed at Sandringham. Its total value is difficult to estimate but experts have said it runs into millions of pounds – and is increasing every year.

## Fashion

When the late Diana, Princess of Wales burst upon the royal scene in 1981, she became a one-woman fashion industry and almost single-handedly revitalised the British millinery business.

Other female members of the Royal Family have set their own styles. The Queen Mother dressed in pastel shades of chiffon and was never seen without a hat; the late Duchess of Kent, Princess Marina, wore a unique shade of blue that became known as

'Marina Blue'; and Princess Anne, when she was younger, was the first Royal lady to appear in public wearing trousers. She is also famous for claiming that 'a good suit can go on for ever, if you have a good hem that can be lowered and raised when necessary'.

## The Queen's Fashion Advisers

The Queen's early designers were Norman Hartnell followed by Hardy Amies, then Ian Thomas became a favourite and, when he retired, his one-time assistant Maureen Rose, took over, becoming a popular designer.

Today, even though Her Majesty still uses the services of mainly British designers, she relies greatly on the advice of her personal assistant, Angela Kelly, who seems to know instinctively what suits her boss. The Queen's more daring choice of colours and fabrics in recent years is largely the result of Miss Kelly's behind-the-scenes influence.

## Finance

The Queen's finances are divided into four separate sources:

1. The Civil List (see Civil List), which meets all expenses Her Majesty incurs as Head of State.
2. The Grant-in-Aid, the amount paid every year by Parliament to the Department of the Environment for the upkeep of the Royal Palaces. Fifty men from the department are employed permanently at Buckingham Palace for the maintenance of the fabric of the building.

3. The Privy Purse, which is financed by the income from the Duchy of Lancaster (see Duchy of Lancaster) and which meets semi-official expenditure of the Sovereign.
4. The private and personal income of the Queen. Only a handful of people know the full extent of Her Majesty's wealth: the Keeper of the Privy Purse, who handles the royal cheque book; the Queen's bankers (see Banks); and possibly her solicitor. But estimates of her worth are said to be wildly exaggerated and one of her former Keepers of the Privy Purse said publicly that she was not among the richest women in the world.

Some people believe the Queen owns all her palaces and castles and every item in the Royal Collection. Of course, she does not. None is held in her own name. They are all inalienable and cannot be sold by her for her personal profit. While nobody would deny that the Queen is a wealthy woman, the palaces, castles and priceless works of art are held by her as Sovereign and will be passed on to her successor in due course.

## Flag Days

There is a great deal of confusion about the days on which official flags are flown and when they are allowed to be flown. The Union Jack (or Union Flag) is flown on all government buildings from 8.00am until sunset on the following days:

## Flying the Union Jack

6 February – The Queen's Accession
19 February – The Duke of York (Prince Andrew's) Birthday
1 March – St David's Day (Flags are flown only in Wales)
10 March – The Earl of Wessex (Prince Edward's) Birthday
2nd Monday in March – Commonwealth Day
21 April – The Queen's Birthday
23 April – St George's Day (Flags are flown only in England)
2 June – Coronation Day
June – The Queen's Official Birthday (As appointed each year)
10 June – The Duke of Edinburgh's Birthday
15 August – The Princess Royal (Princess Anne's) Birthday
2nd Sunday in November – Remembrance Day
14 November – Prince of Wales (Prince Charles's) Birthday
20 November – The Queen and the Duke of Edinburgh's Wedding Anniversary
30 November – St Andrew's Day (Flags are flown only in Scotland)

There is often confusion about the correct way to fly the Union Jack. It should be flown with the cross of St Andrew, the senior, or earlier to be included in the flag, above that of St Patrick, which means at the end next to the flagpole, the broad white stripe goes on top. The flag is composed of three heraldic crosses:

### The Cross of St George
Patron saint of England – a red cross on a white background

### The Cross Saltire of St Andrew
Patron saint of Scotland – a diagonal white cross on a blue background, which was incorporated into the Union Jack in 1606.

### The Cross Saltire of St Patrick

Patron saint of Ireland – a red diagonal cross on a white background.

This was the final emblem to be added to the Union Jack in 1801 and which has been used as the national banner of the United Kingdom ever since.

Wales does not have a separate representation on the flag because when James I came to the throne in 1603, the Principality of Wales was already united with England and was not entitled to its own emblem – the Welsh Dragon.

It was Charles II who declared that the 'Union Flag' should be flown by ships of the Royal Navy as a 'jack' or small standard on board. Hence the reason why the Union Flag has since been known as the Union Jack.

In addition, flags are also flown in London on the day of the State Opening of Parliament. If a building has two or more flagstaffs, it may fly the appropriate national flag, i.e. in Scotland and Wales, as well as the Union Jack, but the national flag must not be given a superior position to the Union Jack.

At Buckingham Palace there is a Flagman, a serving soldier from the Household Division, recommended by his Commanding Officer and working under the supervision of the Master of the Household, whose duties include running the Royal Standard up and down (when the Queen enters and leaves the Palace) and sending off Royal Standards to other destinations when Her Majesty is expected on a visit. His position is on the rooftop of Buckingham Palace and he also travels with the Royal Household to other royal residences.

When he is not busy hoisting and lowering the Standards, he heads a small team of three examining by fluoroscope all mail and parcels that are delivered to the Palace by post, checking to see that nothing dangerous, or even unsuitable, is opened.

There is also a Flagman at Windsor Castle who bears the title of Yeoman of the Royal Tower. He is on duty mainly at weekends when the Queen is in residence and during Ascot Week when the Court moves to Windsor.

## Flying

The Duke of Edinburgh, The Prince of Wales, Prince William, Prince Harry and the Duke of York are all qualified pilots who were awarded their 'wings' during training with the Royal Air Force (the Duke of York was serving in the Royal Navy when he graduated as a helicopter pilot and saw active service in the Falklands Campaign in 1982).

There is now no longer a Queen's Flight; Her Majesty's flying is now carried out by No. 32 (the Royal) Squadron based at Northolt near London. The squadron consists of two BAe 146 jets, each capable of carrying up to twenty-five passengers, and five smaller HS125s with a capacity of seven passengers.

All those involved with flying the Queen and her family are volunteers and are regarded as experts in their field. It is interesting to note that back in 1948 (when it was still The King's Flight), the pilot of Workshop Aircraft Viking VL248 was a certain Flight Lieutenant E.B. Trubshaw, who went on to become one of the most famous fliers in the world as Sir Brian Trubshaw, the chief test pilot of Concorde.

Whenever the Queen is being flown anywhere in the world, there is a 'Purple Carpet' unrolled above, below and in front of her aircraft. This is the term applied by air traffic controllers to the exclusion zone that keeps all other aircraft at a safe distance from the royal flight.

## Food and Drink

Pheasant, partridge, quail, grouse, woodcock and snipe, all shot on one of the royal estates, are served to the Queen and her guests when in season. When Her Majesty and the Duke of Edinburgh dine alone, they rarely eat any red meat these days, so roast beef and Yorkshire pudding is not often on the menu.

Fruit is a royal favourite, with hot-house grapes grown at Windsor used to garnish fish dishes as well as to accompany cheese. Prince Charles prefers fish to meat, with cold dishes such as salmon and prawns high on his list of personal favourites. Nothing containing nuts is allowed on his table and he does not care for chocolate puddings as a dessert, unlike his cousin, the Duke of Gloucester, who is a self-confessed chocoholic, loving it in every form and preferring dark to milk chocolate.

### Her Majesty's Tea

When Her Majesty's 'Calling Tray' is brought at 7.30am every morning, the tea is a special blend made by R. Twining & Company, who happen to be the oldest ratepayers in the City of London, having occupied its premises continuously since1706.

The Queen likes her tea with milk but no sugar; she keeps her own sweetener instead.

The fresh milk comes from the royal dairy at Windsor, and it is said that the first time Her Majesty realised she really was Queen was when she saw her royal cypher 'EIIR' on the milk bottles.

The Duke of Edinburgh prefers coffee, made by the Savoy Hotel Coffee Department.

At breakfast, Her Majesty's honey is supplied by Mr Bruce Gorie from his farm on the Orkney Islands. Frank Cooper Ltd of Esher provides the marmalade Prince Philip likes to spread on his toast, with the bread coming from Justin De Blank in London's Walton Street, where they still bake in the traditional manner in a flat-bottomed oven, overnight.

If sausages are required, very rarely these days, they are bought from Mr Edwin Baxter of Birchington in Kent where they are made from a recipe that has been in the family for more than 130 years. The Queen is the firm's only private customer, but the sausages can be bought from the grocery department at Fortnum & Mason in Piccadilly, the company originally founded by two former royal footmen, and who have been supplying Royalty for more than 150 years.

Smithfield Market in London's East End is the home of J.H. Dewhurst Ltd, supplier of the royal bacon, and the royal fishmonger is Mr Eric Ruffell of Romford. Reckitt & Colman provide the royal tables with mustard.

## Footmen

There are 20 footmen, butlers and, now, female footmen, employed at Buckingham Palace, some of whom move with the Queen to her other residences when required. It is not too difficult to obtain a job as footman as there are often vacancies and the Master of the Household is always on the lookout for suitable candidates. The Palace uses its website to advertise for staff and, even when young men turn up unannounced, they are rarely turned away without an interview.

One of the prime qualifications for a footman is to be of average height and weight: around 5ft 9in tall and with a 36in chest. The reason is that footmen have to fit the uniforms that exist, rather than the other way around. When you realise that the livery worn at State Banquets costs over £2,000 a time, it is not hard to understand why it is worn over and over again. It is believed that some of the outfits date back to the reign of King Edward VII, making them over 100 years old.

Once a footman has been trained and allocated to a post, he works under the supervision of the Pages (see Pages), but the Sergeant Footman, the 'foreman' of the domestic staff, gives him his daily duties. He is the man who first interviewed them when they applied for the job, before passing them on to the next stage, and he gives them numbers, one to six.

Number One gets most of the jobs his seniors hate, such as exercising Her Majesty's Corgis — and cleaning up after them. Number One also carries the 'Calling Trays' for the Queen and the Duke of Edinburgh, with their tea, coffee and biscuits first thing in the morning. But he is not allowed into Her Majesty's bedroom, handing over the tray to her personal maid.

Throughout the day, Number One, working under the Page of the Backstairs, waits in the pantry opposite the Queen's apartment in case he is needed. It can be boring but, as it gives him the opportunity to see Her Majesty at close quarters, the job is seen as a good rung on the career ladder.

Footmen numbers two and four look after the needs of the senior members of the Royal Household, carrying messages between offices and serving coffee when needed.

Number Three is positioned at The King's Door on the west side of the Inner Quadrangle. It is still called The King's Door on the orders of the Queen out of respect for her late father, King George VI. This is the entrance used by the Prime Minister when he arrives for his Tuesday evening audience. Other duties carried out by footman number three include making sure there are plenty of drinks in the Equerries' Withdrawing Room and finding out how many of the Household will be staying in the Palace for luncheon.

Number Five has the worst job of all. He acts as valet to the

Equerry-in-Waiting (see Equerries), cleaning his shoes, inspecting his uniforms for any missing buttons and cleaning and pressing his clothes. As one or two of the men who have held the post of Equerry sometimes get an inflated view of their own importance, they can be very demanding, forgetting that they are all mere servants of the Sovereign; it's just the grade that differs.

Footman number six is called upon to open the car door of any important visitors arriving at the Grand Entrance where he is stationed. It is not a particularly onerous task and can be quite rewarding (see Tipping).

The footmen live on the second floor of Buckingham Palace, with the females in one corner and the men in another. The rooms are comfortably furnished, with a single bed, wardrobe, chest of drawers and easy chair, but there are no en suite bathrooms – they all have to be shared.

The footmen have their rooms cleaned by maids, who also provide fresh bed linen and towels. The laundry, which is free, is collected once a week and they are allowed to invite guests to their rooms, as long as they leave by midnight.

Being a footman is no longer regarded as a job for life, as it once was. Now it is more usually seen as a stepping-stone for something much better paid – and with easier conditions.

## Formality

Formality is taken for granted even today among members of the Royal Family. If, for example, Prince Andrew, Duke of York, is in Buckingham Palace and would like to see his father, the Duke of Edinburgh, he wouldn't dream of simply poking his head around the door and saying hello.

Instead, his private secretary would enquire of his father's private secretary if it might be convenient for him to receive his son. If the answer were in the affirmative, an appointment would be made and entered in the diary. Then, and only then, Andrew would walk to the Duke of Edinburgh's rooms on the first floor where he would be announced with the following words: 'Your Royal Highness, His Royal Highness, the Duke of York.' Andrew would then approach his father, give a short neck-bow and, even in adulthood, probably receive a kiss in return. It is an example of the perfect manners the children show their parents, even in private.

And they also wear 'suitable' clothes when they are going to see either of their parents. Jeans and sweaters are definitely not considered to be acceptable. This formality extends even down to the non-titled members of the family, such as Peter and Zara Phillips, children of the Princess Royal, when they visit their grandparents. It is instilled in them practically from birth.

When Prince William and Prince Harry were very young and they were paraded before their grandparents along with their cousins, all accompanied by their nannies, the order of precedence was strictly adhered to. William and Harry were first in line, followed by Prince Andrew's daughters, then the infant daughter, Louise, of the Earl of Wessex (his second child was not then born) carried in the arms of her nanny bringing up the rear. Nobody saw anything strange in this, it was simply the way things were, and are, done in the Royal Family.

## Forms of Address

On being presented to the Queen (one is 'presented' not 'introduced', as it is assumed everyone will know who she is), she is addressed initially as 'Your Majesty' and thereafter as 'Ma'am' (to rhyme with 'ham' not 'smarm').

The Duke of Edinburgh, the Prince of Wales, the Duke of York, the Earl of Wessex and the Princess Royal are all addressed as 'Your Royal Highness', then 'Sir' or 'Ma'am'.

It is considered courteous for ladies to give a short curtsey and gentlemen a short neck-bow (King George V said only head waiters should bow from the waist) when meeting members of the Royal Family, but these days the Queen and her family are very relaxed about the conventions and do not insist if anyone prefers not to 'bow or bob'.

When writing to the Queen, the greeting should be 'Madam' (not 'Dear Madam'). And, at the end of the letter, above one's own signature should be the words 'I have the honour to remain Your Majesty's humble and obedient Servant . . .' and always handwritten, even if the rest of the letter has been typed, and preferably using a fountain pen, not a ballpoint.

## Funerals

It may sound macabre, but the preliminary arrangements for the Queen's funeral began even before her father, King George VI, was buried on 16 February 1952. All members of the Royal Family are given code names for their funerals. The Queen's is 'London Bridge'; the Duke of Edinburgh's is listed under 'Forth Bridge'. The late Queen Mother's funeral came under the code name 'Tay Bridge'.

For an event such as Her Majesty's funeral, no detail is overlooked, and every year since the accession a working group of six people from the Lord Chamberlain's Office and the College of Arms meets to update the copious file under the chairmanship of the Earl Marshal, the Duke of Norfolk. As the United Kingdom's premier duke, he has overall responsibility for all the arrangements for the Sovereign's funeral. As the years pass, there are obviously changes in the personnel who are to be on duty on the day, and also the requirements of the media have to be taken into consideration.

When the Queen first came to the Throne, it would not have been necessary to accommodate television cameras as it was thought the occasion would be far too solemn for such an intrusion. Today it would be unthinkable for the Sovereign's funeral not to be televised live with cameras and microphones, complete with a battery of commentators stationed at strategic points within Westminster Abbey and along the processional route.

There is a long-established blueprint for these preparations, dating back to 1901 and the State funeral of Queen Victoria, which was the first of a British Sovereign to be held in daytime. Before this, all royal funerals were held privately at night with little ceremonial attached.

The funeral preceding Queen Victoria's was that of King William IV who had died some 64 years earlier, in 1837.

It wasn't until 1936, when the Queen's grandfather, George V, was buried, that the BBC was allowed to broadcast the sounds of the marching men and the solemn beat of the drums along the route. But even then there was no question of allowing microphones inside Westminster Abbey for the service.

The details for the Sovereign's funeral include who is to be invited, Heads of State and the remaining Monarchs, their transport to the United Kingdom and where they are to be accommodated. The seating plan inside the Abbey is a delicate and complicated arrangement with the order of precedence strictly adhered to. Then the number of troops taking part and their place in the funeral procession has to be decided, taking into consideration military requirements for active service overseas.

The regiments of which the Queen is Colonel-in-Chief are given priority, while the privilege of hauling the gun-carriage on which the royal coffin is carried rests with the Royal Navy, who jealously guard the honour. This tradition dates from the funeral of Queen Victoria, when the lead horses of the Royal Artillery suddenly panicked and broke the traces, so the naval guard of honour stepped in and physically took over the task of pulling the gun-carriage, and they have done so ever since. Such is the way in which certain royal traditions have their origin.

## Protocol for the Queen's Funeral

On the death of the Sovereign, the coffin is first taken to Westminster Hall at the Houses of Parliament for the Lying-in-State. Male members of the Royal family stand guard as the rest of the family and the Royal Household file slowly past to pay their last respects followed by the general public for several days. This part of the funeral arrangements comes under the supervision of the Lord Great Chamberlain, the Hereditary Keeper of the Palace of Westminster.

Once the Lying-in-State is completed, 150 naval ratings then pull the gun-carriage across the road to Westminster Abbey and, after the funeral service, to Paddington Station from where the coffin, accompanied by the chief mourners will depart on the Royal Train, with all blinds drawn, for the final interment in St George's Chapel, Windsor. The final resting place is in the royal vault where the words to be engraved have been agreed by the Queen many years before.

At regular intervals, there are rehearsals for the Sovereign's funeral, with the Crown Equerry, who is responsible for all royal travel on land, checking each segment of the journeys, stopwatch in hand. The Yeomen of the Guard, Heralds and every member of the Ecclesiastical Household in England and Scotland know exactly what they have to do, where they stand and at what time.

The Queen has approved the type of coffin to be used – it will be lead-lined and she sees nothing melancholy in being made aware of such details; to her, it is just another aspect of her role as Head of State.

Once the working group has finalised its plans, they are submitted to a much larger committee, including representatives of the Prime Minister, the Ministry of Defence, (Army, Royal Navy,

Royal Air Force and Royal Marines), the various police forces and local and national railway authorities in London and Windsor and the Department of the Environment plus the Commonwealth Secretariat, all of whom are involved to a greater or lesser extent.

Attention to detail is a byword in the Royal Household and it is because of this that every royal ceremonial occasion, including funerals, is carried out with military-like precision and discipline. Perfection is the only standard.

## Gardeners

On the anniversary of the Coronation, and one or two other important occasions, The Worshipful Company of Gardeners (founded in 1605) presents flowers to the Queen in spite of the fact that she did not carry flowers at her Coronation, as she had both hands full carrying the Orb and Sceptre. However, she did accept a small bouquet of mixed white flowers to carry on her way to Westminster Abbey.

The Company has traditionally provided the flowers for royal weddings, including that of the then Princess Elizabeth and the Duke of Edinburgh in 1947, the Silver Wedding anniversaries of King George V and Queen Mary in 1935, and King George VI and Queen Elizabeth in 1948, as well as the weddings of Princess Anne and Captain Mark Phillips in 1973, and that of the Prince and Princess of Wales in 1981. Small posies are also offered at all royal christenings.

Since 1954, the Master of the Worshipful Company has presented flowers to Her Majesty personally every five years. In other years, the flowers are simply delivered to Buckingham Palace.

Every afternoon, when the Queen is at Buckingham Palace, she likes to walk in the gardens after luncheon (she never uses the diminutive 'lunch', believing it to be vulgar). The unwritten rule for the Household is to remain out of sight as Her Majesty calls this her 'thinking time' and she likes to be alone. The exception to the rule is the team of Palace gardeners. They are permitted to remain working and, often, the Queen will pause and chat to them about the various plants and flowers. If she doesn't stop, they will remove any headgear they may be wearing, give a short neck-bow and carry on once she has passed by.

## Garden Parties

Every July, the Queen holds four Garden Parties – or, to give them their official title: Afternoon Parties. Three are held in the grounds of Buckingham Palace and a further one at the Palace of Holyroodhouse in Edinburgh, when the Court is in residence in Scotland. In London, around 9,000 guests are invited, with 4,000 in Edinburgh.

### How to Obtain an Invitation to a Royal Garden Party

It is possible to write and ask the Lord Chamberlain, but this avenue is rarely successful. Lord Lieutenants, High Sheriffs, Lord Mayors, Mayors and other civic leaders together with those who run various charitable organisations are given an allocation and they are permitted to submit names to the Palace for approval. The Lord Chamberlain's Office in conjunction with the Master of the Household's Department organises the parties.

A complete list of every person who has ever been invited and who has attended or declined an invitation is maintained on a computer.

The invitations are hand written by a group of ladies who work under the quaint title of Temporary Lady Clerks, but it takes so long for the invitations to be written and checked to make sure every name, title and decoration is correct that the lady clerks work all year round in an office in St James's Palace.

The rules governing who is allowed to attend state that each invitation is usually addressed to the lady of the house (they have replaced the old-style 'coming out' balls when young débutantes were presented at Court by their mothers) and that unmarried daughters aged 18 and over may accompany their mother, but not sons.

The invitation is written on a stiff pasteboard card, which states:

*The Lord Chamberlain is commanded by*
*Her Majesty to invite*

(names of invitees)

*to a Garden Party at Buckingham Palace*
*on (date) from 4pm to 6pm.*

In the lower left-hand corner are the words: 'Morning Dress, Uniform or Lounge Suit'. In the early days of the Queen's reign, it would have been unthinkable for any gentleman to wear anything but morning dress, but Her Majesty insisted that lounge suits should be permitted when the guest lists were extended to include men and women from all walks of life and every class, and she was anxious that none of her guests would decline her invitation simply because they could not afford formal wear.

Ladies wear elegant dresses and hats, and while trouser suits are tolerated, they are not generally favoured. Ladies who 'know the form' wear comfortable shoes, as high heels can be tricky on the lawns.

Accompanying the invitation is a map showing the three entrances to Buckingham Palace: one is the Grand Entrance, which first-timers should always use as it may be the only time they actually get to go inside the Palace proper; the other two lead directly into the 40-acre gardens where the party is to take place.

The gates are opened at 3.35pm and old hands (leading politicians, diplomats and bishops receive an invitation every year) usually head for the tea marquees that are arranged along the south boundary. They know the newcomers will usually wait until they see the Queen, by which time there will be an almighty crush.

Several varieties of tea are provided but, on warm afternoons, the most popular beverage is iced coffee. Finger sandwiches, cakes, sticky buns and gateaux are served but there are never enough chairs and tables to go around, so handling cups, saucers and plates while standing requires a certain dexterity.

At 4.00pm precisely, the Queen, accompanied by the Duke of

Edinburgh, appears through the glass doors of the Bow Room and stands at the top of the Garden Steps while one of the two military bands on duty plays the National Anthem. The Royal Family then splits up and each one takes a separate 'lane' down which they walk slowly, stopping occasionally to talk with one or two guests who have been selected previously by gentlemen attendants. This selection has nothing to do with rank or title, but simply because it is felt the Queen would like to meet that particular person. It may be because they are wearing an unusual outfit, national dress or uniform, or because they have indicated that they were invited because of some service to the community that has been rewarded with this invitation.

The Queen's 'lane' is easy to identify, as hers is the only one lined by Yeomen of the Guard in their Tudor uniforms.

Her Majesty's destination is the Royal Tea Marquee some 300 yards away. It takes an hour for the Queen to make the journey; meanwhile the rest of the Royal Family, working their own 'lanes', manage to arrive at exactly the same moment.

The Royal Tea Tent is open only to those with special invitations: diplomats, archbishops and senior politicians, and a semi-circle of chairs has been arranged at a discreet distance from the tent so that a small number of guests can watch, from a respectful range, the Queen and her VIP guests taking their tea.

At 5.30pm on the dot, Her Majesty walks slowly back to the Palace and for the guests that is it. The Garden Party is over for another year.

## Garter Service

The Garter Service takes place on the Monday of Royal Ascot Week in June. The Order of the Garter is the most important order of chivalry in England (in Scotland it is the Order of the Thistle) and is limited to 24 Knights Companion, plus extra royal Knights and Ladies who normally use the initials LG after their name. However, when the Princess Royal was made a Lady of the Garter, she asked her mother for permission, which was immediately granted, to use the male KG instead.

A new knight is invested by the Queen, who buckles a garter to his left leg. Then, after a celebration luncheon, the Knights all process to St George's Chapel for the full ceremonial installation. Included in the procession are the Military Knights of Windsor and the Yeomen of the Guard, with the Knights wearing plumed hats, blue mantles and a dark-blue garter worn below the left knee. Ladies wear the garter on the upper left arm.

Inside St George's Chapel, each knight has his or her own stall bearing their coat of arms in a magnificent heraldic display. The motto of the Order is '*Honi soit qui mal y pense*' ('Evil be to him who evil thinks'). This romantic saying is credited to Edward III, founder of the Order in 1348, when he was said to have retrieved the garter of a lady at Court when she accidentally lost it, causing merriment to onlookers and embarrassment to her.

The Garter Service inside the chapel is not usually open to the public but it is possible to see the procession from the Middle and Lower Wards of the Castle by applying to The Lord Chamberlain's Office, St James's Palace, London SW1A 1BE.

If one is successful in the ballot (and there are so many applications this is the only fair method of selection) the tickets are posted several weeks before the event.

## Gentlemen at Arms

Her Majesty's Body Guard of the Honourable Corps of Gentlemen at Arms is the senior royal bodyguard and the 'Nearest Guard', which means they are privileged to be allowed to stand guard nearest to the Sovereign on State occasions such as the State

Opening of Parliament, the coronation and at royal funerals. At the Lying-in-State of the Sovereign, the entire Corps has the right to stand watch over the coffin in the Palace of Westminster.

Originally created by Henry VIII in 1509, today the Corps consists of five Officers and twenty-seven Gentlemen. The Captain, a political appointment, heads them, as he is the Government Chief Whip in the House of Lords, so changes with each Government. His badge of office is a gold stick with his uniform (as well as those of the Corps) being a red-skirted coat with Garter blue velvet cuffs, embroidered with the Tudor royal badge of the Portcullis. A gold, oak-leaf design pouch belt and heavy gold epaulettes are worn, with helmets adorned with white feathers (the helmets are worn every time the Corps is on duty, even in church). Swords are worn but never drawn and the Gentlemen also carry ceremonial battle-axes, which are normally kept in the Corps' headquarters at Engine Court in St James's Palace.

The executive officers of the Corps are the Lieutenant, the Standard Bearer (this reflects the fact that they were originally a mounted corps, otherwise they would carry a colour), the Clerk of the Cheque and Harbinger, the man who in ancient times would have preceded the Corps to make arrangements for accommodation and food.

Only two females have been appointed to be Captain of the Corps. When they took up office, the Queen agreed that she would not be required to wear the uniform; instead, they were given a brooch of office. However they did carry the Gold Stick.

## George Cross and George Medal

Both the George Cross and the George Medal were instituted on 24 September 1940 on the orders of King George VI to reward 'the many acts of heroism performed by both male and female persons especially during the present war' (the Second World War, 1939–45).

The Cross is available to male and female civilians and persons regardless of rank in the Armed Services, including Military

Nursing Services and Women's Auxiliary Services, and also to members of Commonwealth countries.

The first awards for both the Cross and the Medal were gazetted on 30 September 1940 and, in 1942, the King declared that the island of Malta should be awarded the George Cross in recognition of its inhabitants' fortitude and bravery during devastating and constant bombing by the German Luftwaffe. It was the only occasion when an entire population was awarded the decoration.

The George Medal was awarded to members of Dover Fire Service in 1940, following a large-scale attack on the docks when many fires were started in ships and oil storage areas.

The first woman to be awarded the George Cross was Mrs Odette Sansom, a British undercover agent working behind enemy lines in France. She was captured and tortured and finally executed by the Nazis and her family later received the award on her behalf at Buckingham Palace.

The Queen, as fount of all honours, awards the decorations on the advice of the Prime Minister, the Secretary of State for Defence, or, for members of Commonwealth countries, the appropriate Secretary of State.

Holders of the George Cross are given an annuity of £100 for life; if the award is made posthumously, their estate is granted a £50 annuity.

The insignia of the George Cross is a plain silver cross, with a circular medallion in the centre depicting a design of St George and the Dragon, with the inscription 'For Gallantry' around the medallion. The reverse is plain and bears the name of the recipient and the date of the award. The Cross is worn suspended from a dark-blue ribbon.

The George Medal is circular in shape and made of silver. On the obverse is the crowned effigy of the Sovereign, with St George slaying the Dragon on the reverse. The words 'The George Medal' is engraved and the ribbon is red with five narrow stripes of blue.

The George Cross is worn immediately after the Victoria Cross but before all Orders of Chivalry and other decorations and, since 1971, all holders of the former Albert and Edward Medals have been permitted to exchange their decorations for the George Cross.

In 1974, James Beaton, Princess Anne's personal protection officer, foiled a kidnap attempt in The Mall, during which he was shot five times. For his bravery and dedication to duty, the Queen awarded him the George Cross, the highest award possible for a civilian during peacetime.

## Gurkha Orderly Officers

The Queen is a great admirer of the Gurkha Regiment and, since 1954, she has always had two Gurkha officers in permanent attendance. They can be seen closely following Her Majesty when she holds an Investiture at the Palace (the first occasion was on 6 July 1954) and they also appear at other ceremonial functions. It was Queen Victoria who first commanded Indian officers to attend her in 1876, when she became Empress of India and they have been in attendance continually since that time.

The officers arrive in England to attend an English language course at the Army School of Languages in Beaconsfield, Buckinghamshire, before taking up their posting at Buckingham Palace, usually in March, when they relieve their predecessors.

The Queen rewards her Gurkha officers by making them Members of the Royal Victorian Order, her personal order of chivalry. The Prince of Wales is Colonel-in-Chief of 2nd King Edward VII's Own Goorkas (there are several spellings of the name) and he retains on his staff a Gurkha Orderly who is seconded for a two-year appointment.

## Gifts

Men, women and children from all over the world like to show their feelings towards Royalty by sending them presents – at Christmas and on their birthdays. Every year, the Queen receives hundreds of boxes of chocolates from well-meaning but ill-advised donors. She does not taste even one. Every gift of food and drink sent to any member of the Royal Family is immediately destroyed because of the ever-present possibility it might contain poison.

In the early years of the reign, the gifts were distributed to hospitals and schools. Sadly, that is no longer possible in the current climate of terrorist threats. Gifts of hand-knitted baby clothes are often sent to royal mothers. These are sent on to deserving charities, as there is little danger of contamination. And every gift that is received at the Palace is acknowledged with a letter thanking the donor for their kindness.

Many people ask what is the most popular present the Queen has ever received. The answer is surprisingly simple. One of Her Majesty's oldest friends once asked Prince Philip what he thought his wife might like to receive as a gift and he replied it was a plastic, transparent umbrella costing just £11. Apparently, the Queen Mother always liked to carry one so that she could see out when it rained and, more importantly, that she could be seen. The Queen thought this was an excellent idea and when she, too, received one she was delighted, and today she has a number of these umbrellas, all trimmed in various colours to match her outfit of the day.

## Godparents

At their Christening (see Christenings), the Godparents of the various members of the Royal Family were as follows:

The Queen (as Princess Elizabeth)     *King George V and Queen Mary*
*The Earl of Strathmore and Kinghorne*
*Mary, the Princess Royal*

|                         | *Lady Elphinstone*<br>*Prince Arthur, Duke of Connaught* |
|-------------------------|-----------------------------------------------------------|
| Prince Charles          | *King George VI*<br>*Queen Mary*<br>*Princess Margaret*<br>*Victoria, Dowager Countess of Milford Haven*<br>*The Hon. David Bowes-Lyon*<br>*Lady Brabourne (now Countess Mountbatten of Burma)*<br>*King Haakon of Norway* [did not attend service]<br>*Prince George of Greece* [did not attend service] |
| Princess Anne           | *Queen Elizabeth (later the Queen Mother)*<br>*Princess Andrew of Greece*<br>*Princess Margarita of Hohenlohe-Langenburg*<br>*Earl Mountbatten of Burma*<br>*Rev the Hon Andrew Elphinstone* |
| Prince Andrew           | *Prince Henry, Duke of Gloucester*<br>*Princess Alexandra*<br>*Lord Elphinstone*<br>*The Earl of Euston*<br>*Mrs Harold Phillips* |
| Prince Edward           | *Prince Richard of Gloucester (now Duke of Gloucester)*<br>*The Duchess of Kent*<br>*The Earl of Snowdon*<br>*Princess George of Hanover*<br>*Prince Louis of Hesse* |
| Prince William of Wales | *King Constantine II of the Hellenes* |

|                                  |                                                              |
|----------------------------------|--------------------------------------------------------------|
|                                  | *Lord Romsey (now Lord Brabourne)*                           |
|                                  | *Sir Laurens van der Post*                                   |
|                                  | *Princess Alexandra*                                         |
|                                  | *The Duchess of Westminster*                                 |
|                                  | *Lady Susan Hussey*                                          |
| Prince Henry (Harry) of Wales    | *The Duke of York*                                           |
|                                  | *Lady Sarah Armstrong-Jones (now Lady Chatto)*               |
|                                  | *Lady Vestey*                                                |
|                                  | *Mrs William Bartholomew*                                    |
|                                  | *Mr Bryan Organ*                                             |
|                                  | *Mr Gerald Ward*                                             |
| Princess Beatrice of York        | *Viscount Linley*                                            |
|                                  | *Peter Palumbo*                                              |
|                                  | *The Duchess of Roxburghe*                                   |
|                                  | *Mrs Harry Cottrell*                                         |
|                                  | *Mrs John Greenall*                                          |
| Princess Eugenie of York         | *James Ogilvy*                                               |
|                                  | *Captain Alastair Ross*                                      |
|                                  | *Mrs Ronald Ferguson*                                        |
|                                  | *Mrs Patrick Dodd-Noble*                                     |
|                                  | *Miss Louise Blacker*                                        |
| Lady Louise Windsor              | *Lord Ivar Mountbatten*                                      |
|                                  | *Lady Alexandra Hetherington*                                |
|                                  | *Lady Sarah Chatto*                                          |
|                                  | *Mrs Urs Schwarzenbach*                                      |
|                                  | *Mr Rupert Elliott*                                          |
| Viscount Severn                  | *Major Alistair Bruce*                                       |
|                                  | *Mr Duncan Bullivant*                                        |
|                                  | *Mr Thomas Hill*                                             |
|                                  | *Mrs Mark Poulton*                                           |
|                                  | *Miss Jeanye Irwin*                                          |

## Grace-and-Favour Residences

These are some of the most desirable houses and apartments in the country, all owned by the Crown, with the tenancy granted by the Queen. Since the reign of George III, these properties have been allocated to 'deserving' people such as distinguished officers in the Army, Royal Air Force or Royal Navy, and also to those who are considered to have given service to the Crown.

In London, there are apartments in St James's Palace and Kensington Palace (but not in Buckingham Palace). There is also a private house in Grosvenor Street, SW1. Both Windsor Castle and Hampton Court Palace contain grace-and-favour homes with some of the large, draughty apartments at Hampton Court being occupied by the widows of former senior Court officials. What they lack in comfort, they make up for in having a prestigious address.

There is one particularly attractive property opposite the maze at Hampton Court, known as Wilderness House, which contains not only extensive living accommodation, but also its own ballroom.

There is only one grace-and-favour residence in Scotland. It is The Queen's House at 36 Moray Place, Edinburgh, and there are none in Wales or Northern Ireland.

Current members of the Royal Household can be offered houses and apartments for the duration of their employment, but they are required to pay up to 17 per cent of their salary as rent. The remainder of the grace-and-favour residences are usually rent-free, though at the time of writing, Prince and Princess Michael of Kent are expected to be asked to pay the commercial rate for their apartment in Kensington Palace – around £120,000 a year.

The most elegant of all Grace-and-Favour homes is Clarence House, where the Prince of Wales and the Duchess of Cornwall have their London residence. It, too, is rent-free, but His Royal Highness does pay for the upkeep apart from structural maintenance, which is paid by the Royal Household.

## Handbags

Wherever the Queen goes in the world the 'Brown Bag' goes with her. This is not the handbag without which she is rarely seen in public, but an extra that members of the Royal Household carry with essentials such as an additional pair of shoes, stockings, gloves (HM can wear up to five pairs a day) and any other items necessary for a woman's daily needs. The bag is always close by so that in an emergency anything needed can be produced without delay.

On one occasion, during a visit to the USA, the 'Brown Bag' was left on the aircraft and an airman retrieved it, only to be told to 'hand it over' by a member of the Royal Household, who, in turn, gave it to one of the Queen's personal staff (female) so that the item, if required, could be passed to her by another woman. The inference was that items of a personal nature must be handled only by a female.

## Heights

The height of members of the Royal Family is as follows:

| | |
|---|---|
| The Queen | 5ft 4in (1.62m) |
| Prince Philip | 5ft 11in (1.80m) |
| The Prince of Wales | 5ft 9in (1.75m) |
| Prince William | 6ft 2in (1.88m) |
| Prince Harry | 6ft 2in (1.88m) |
| Prince Andrew, Duke of York | 6ft (1.83m) |
| Prince Edward, Earl of Wessex | 6ft 1in (1.85m) |
| The Princess Royal | 5ft 6in (1.68m) |
| The late Diana, Princess of Wales | 5ft 10in (1.78m) |

## Heir Apparent and Heir Presumptive

The eldest son of the Sovereign is always the Heir Apparent, and were he to die before succeeding to the Throne, his eldest son would become Heir Apparent. So, Prince Charles is Heir Apparent to Elizabeth II and, were he to die before his mother, Prince William of Wales would become Heir Apparent.

The difference between 'Apparent' and 'Presumptive' is that the Heir Presumptive is the next in line to the throne whose right to succeed could be overturned by the birth of someone with a superior right. For example, from 1936 to 1952, Princess Elizabeth was Heir Presumptive because there was no male child with a greater claim. However, if her parents, King George VI and Queen Elizabeth, had subsequently had a son, even if he had been 20 years younger, he would have become Heir Apparent as male children take precedence over their female siblings at all times.

## High Sheriffs

Although the office of High Sheriff was extremely important hundreds of years ago, when its holder was the representative of the Monarch in the shires and became responsible for local administration, today the office is purely ceremonial, having little to do with any matters of significance and is regarded mainly as a decorative addition to civic dignity. The sole public duty remaining is that of returning officer in parliamentary elections with the occasional additional task of enforcing certain High Court orders. The office is held for one year only and still has a certain social status attached, so it is quite highly sought-after.

One prerequisite for would-be candidates is possession of a large property suitable for entertaining, so an equally large bank balance comes in handy. The selection of the High Sheriff takes place during a meeting of the Privy Council, when the successful candidates name is 'pricked' by the Queen with a brass-handled bodkin. The instrument dates from the reign of Elizabeth I, who apparently used her sewing bodkin on one occasion when she did not have a pen.

Every county in England and Wales has a High Sheriff, but those appointed for the Duchy of Lancaster are 'pricked' in a private ceremony during an audience of the Queen with the Chancellor of the Duchy. Similarly, the Prince of Wales, as Duke of Cornwall, 'pricks' the High Sheriffs of the Duchy of Cornwall at a meeting of the Prince's Council in November each year.

High Sheriffs wear a uniform, which they have to buy themselves, consisting of short, black, velvet tailcoat, white lace jabot, black, knee-length breeches and black stockings, with black, patent-leather, buckled shoes.

## Homeopathy

Both the Queen and the Prince of Wales are enthusiasts for complementary medicine; the practice of treating 'like with like', now known as homeopathy. They are by no means the first or only Royals to support this form of medicine. As early as the mid-19th century, Queen Adelaide, consort of William IV, was treated by this method and, since then, kings, queens, princes and princesses have all been interested in homeopathy.

The philosophy is that by administering diluted doses of substances that can cause the illness or condition in the first place, a 'natural' cure is effected. Practitioners of the method use only natural substances as opposed to chemical drugs.

The Queen's grandfather, King George V, was a firm believer in homeopathy as was his son, King George VI, who not only named one of his racehorses Hypericum after a natural remedy, he granted the title 'Royal' to the London Homeopathic Hospital, of which the Queen is now Patron.

Her Majesty has been known to use homeopathic remedies on her dogs as well as taking them herself as a means of promoting the body's natural healing and feeling of well-being. Whenever she, and the Prince of Wales, travel abroad, their accompanying physicians, who are orthodox doctors, make sure a case of homeopathic medicines is in the luggage.

## Housekeepers

There is a resident housekeeper in each of the Queen's homes. Their job is to supervise the domestic arrangements such as cleaning, laundry and vacuuming (newcomers are given special instruction in how to use a vacuum correctly; i.e. always walking backwards to avoid leaving footmarks on the carpet). Buckingham Palace has a total of 26 housemaids under the control of Her Majesty's Chief Housekeeper, who, in the early days of the reign, was invariably given the courtesy title 'Mrs' whatever her marital state. That custom has now been done away with.

## Holyroodhouse, Hereditary Keeper

The title of Hereditary Keeper of the Palace of Holyroodhouse, the Sovereign's official residence in Edinburgh, has been in the possession of the Duke of Hamilton, Scotland's premier peer, since 10 November 1646, when it was granted by Charles I. The original Duke's successors have held the title unbroken since that date.

The Keeper holds the keys to the Palace and, on the arrival of the Sovereign, or the High Commissioner of the Church of Scotland (see High Commissioner), he offers them symbolically to illustrate their right to the Palace.

The Keeper occupies apartments on the fourth floor of Holyroodhouse, which are decorated with Hamilton family portraits. The apartments are for the sole use of the Duke and his family except when the Queen or the High Commissioner requires them. His duties include being in attendance on Her Majesty when she is in residence and he has the power to appoint a Deputy Keeper and the Bailie and Clerk of the Abbey Court, all of whom are appointed on an unpaid basis.

The day-to-day organisation is left in the hands of the Superintendent of the Palace.

## HRH

In 1917 King George V restricted the use of the title His (or Her) Royal Highness, Prince or Princess, to the children of the Sovereign, the children of the sons of the Sovereign, and the eldest son of the eldest son of the Prince of Wales. Their wives would also be known as HRH. So, if Prince William should marry while his father is still Prince of Wales, William's wife would be HRH and their eldest son would also be a prince and bear the style HRH, but not any subsequent children (unless the Queen decided otherwise.)

The husband and children of the daughters of the Sovereign are not entitled to be either Prince or Princess or to be styled HRH. So, even though the Queen wanted Princess Anne's children to be given titles, but she didn't, they were not entitled to be either Prince Peter or Princess Zara. Neither was Mark Phillips, the Princess's first husband, nor Tim Laurence, her second, allowed to be HRH.

King George VI made a special dispensation when Princess Elizabeth married Lieutenant Philip Mountbatten in 1947, to permit his son-in-law to be called HRH the Duke of Edinburgh, as he did not want his daughter marrying a commoner. However, he refused to create him a Prince of the United Kingdom, a title the Queen bestowed on him in 1957.

## Current Entitlement to the HRH Style

Queen Elizabeth II
The Prince of Wales
The Duchess of Cornwall
Prince William of Wales
Prince Henry (Harry) of Wales
Prince Andrew, Duke of York
Princess Beatrice of York
Princess Eugenie of York
Prince Edward, Earl of Wessex
The Countess of Wessex
The Princess Royal
The Duke and Duchess of Gloucester
The Duke and Duchess of Kent
Prince and Princess Michael of Kent
Princess Alexandra

The children of Prince Edward, Earl of Wessex, Viscount [James] Severn and Lady Louise are not styled HRH or Prince or Princess at their parents' request, and with the agreement of the Queen.

The wife of a Sovereign is styled Her Majesty, but the husband of a Queen Regnant e.g. Queen Victoria and Elizabeth II, is not called His Majesty. Queen Victoria's husband, Albert, was already a Prince when they married and he was styled HRH.

# J

## Inheritance Duties and Income Tax

None of the Queen's wealth or property is liable to death duties or inheritance duty as it is now called, as all tax is raised in the Queen's name and is therefore not raised against the Sovereign. So her heirs will be able to inherit a sizable fortune intact. However, every other member of the Royal Family is liable to pay tax – or death duties – as they are treated as private citizens in this matter.

Until February 1993, the Queen, as Monarch, was exempt from paying income tax on both her Civil List allowance and on her personal assets. However, she informed the then Prime Minister, John Major, that she intended voluntarily to pay income tax for the first time. She isn't the first Sovereign to pay tax; Queen Victoria, King Edward VII and King George V had all paid some form of income tax during their time on the throne, albeit in the days when income tax was just a few pence in the pound, rather than the punitive amounts of later years.

We are never going to know how much the Queen pays, as her affairs, in line with every other private individual, are confidential and are never revealed in Palace accounts, but it is generally accepted that she is a higher-rate tax payer. However, Her Majesty is also liable to pay tax on her private estates at Sandringham and Balmoral – and she does pay any tax due to Customs and Excise on gifts she receives while she is on overseas visits. She is also registered for Value Added Tax through the Duchy of Lancaster.

All other members of the Royal Family are liable to pay tax on their incomes from all sources.

## Information and Correspondence

The Queen receives over 1,000 letters every week, and each one is carefully read and given a reply.

There is a special section within the Private Secretary's Office that deals with all the letters that arrive addressed to Her Majesty – between 200 and 300 a day, rising to over 1,000 a day on special occasions such as royal births, weddings or funerals.

The letters (and e-mails) come from many different types of person, and are on a wide variety of subjects. Children write asking for information about certain aspects of royal life: how many dogs does the Queen have and what are their names...who looks after Her Majesty's horses...what sort of car does she drive? Other letters tell of personal problems and ask for help, either on behalf of themselves or members of their family or friends.

If the letter is a complaint about something the Government has done, or neglected to do, it is passed to the appropriate Government department for reply. Anything relating to a Commonwealth country goes to the Governor-General of the country concerned. Nothing is ever ignored; everyone receives an acknowledgement.

The replies are signed on behalf of Her Majesty by one of her three Private Secretaries, or, if children or the elderly have written them, one of the Ladies-in-Waiting will write a more personal letter.

The section also answers queries that are phoned in by the public but not those from the media; all media requests are directed to the Press Office.

Another of the responsibilities of this section is to send out on behalf of the Queen over 13,000 messages of congratulation to those men and women who are either celebrating their Diamond Wedding Anniversary or a 100th birthday (see Birthdays).

Finally, one of the important daily tasks of this department is to produce the Court Circular (see Court Circular) for distribution to newspapers such as the *Times,* the *Daily Telegraph,* the *Independent* and the *Scotsman.*

## Investiture of the Prince of Wales

Although wide coverage on television, radio and the press was given to the Investiture of Prince Charles as Prince of Wales on 1 July 1969 in Caernarvon Castle, the ceremony itself is comparatively modern in royal terms.

It was in 1911 that Prince Edward (later King Edward VIII), son of King George V, was invested, again at Caernarvon, as Prince of Wales, in a ceremony devised entirely at the behest of the flamboyant Welsh politician David Lloyd George, who saw it as a public relations coup. There had been previous investitures of Princes of Wales with the first, Edward of Caernarvon, being invested before Parliament at Lincoln on 7 February 1301, and another was of Prince George (later George II) in 1714.

Prince Charles was only ten years old when he was created the 21st Prince of Wales on 26 July 1958, and the recorded announcement was heard by thousands of people at Cardiff Arms Park during the final day of the 1958 Empire Games (the last Games to be called 'Empire', as these competitions have since been renamed the Commonwealth Games). The Investiture took place 11 years later and was a bi-lingual ceremony (English–Welsh) with Prince Charles, who had studied the language briefly at the University College of Wales, Aberystwyth, making his responses in both tongues. The Home Secretary, James Callaghan, and the Secretary of State for Wales, George Thomas (later Viscount Tonypandy) read the letters patent; one in English, and the latter in Welsh.

Once the newly invested Prince of Wales had uttered his Oath of Allegiance to Her Majesty, she and the Duke of Edinburgh conducted him to Queen Eleanor's Gate, the King's Gate and the steps leading to the lower ward of the castle to present him to the people of Wales for the first time as their new Prince of Wales.

The event, organised by the Queen's brother-in-law, the Earl of Snowdon, had been televised by the BBC and ITV, with reporters and commentators from all over the world, including the actor Richard Burton and playwright Emlyn Williams, and the total worldwide audience was estimated to be in excess of 200 million.

# J

## Jewel House

The Crown Jewels are housed in the Jewel House in the Waterloo Block of the Tower of London. They are on display over two floors, with the most valuable contained in a strong room in the basement, and the coronation ceremonial robes, medals and decorations kept in display cabinets on the floor above, all protected behind reinforced glass, with the latest security equipment installed.

It is impossible accurately to estimate the total value of the Crown Jewels as, not only the intrinsic quality of the gold and gems in the insignia must be counted but also the royal provenance. And, strange as it may seem, none is insured, for a very simple and logical reason: they are irreplaceable, so there is little point in trying to insure something that cannot be replaced, and this is another reason why they are guarded so closely. However, they are covered by something called a Government Indemnity, which means the Government would have to replace any stolen or damaged items of the Crown Jewels. Similarly, the most important artefacts in the Royal Collection are covered by the same indemnity. However, when paintings and other works of art are loaned to outside exhibitions, one of the conditions is that the borrowers must fully insure them and pay the premiums.

The Keeper of the Jewel House is also the Resident Governor of the Tower and the post has traditionally been held by a former senior army officer.

Until 1990, the Keeper was a member of the Royal

Household but, in that year, the Historic Royal Palaces Agency assumed control of the Tower of London (and the Jewel House) and the Keeper is no longer part of the Royal Household.

The Jewel House troop of wardens patrol the Jewel House, wearing royal livery and, as part of the Tower, the exhibition is open to the public throughout the year. It is regarded as one of the top tourist attractions in London.

## Jubilees

The Queen's Silver Jubilee (25 years) was celebrated on 6 February 1977 with church services throughout the country. Then, later in the year, Her Majesty and Prince Philip embarked on 6 tours of the United Kingdom during which they visited 36 counties followed by visits to several Commonwealth countries covering more than 56,000 miles in all.

On 7 June, the Queen drove in the Gold State Coach to St Paul's Cathedral for a Jubilee Service attended by members of the Royal Family, Ambassadors, leading politicians and High Commissioners. Outside, thousands of people lined the streets to cheer the procession that was seen on television by an audience estimated to be over 500 million.

Street parties were held in cities, towns and villages around the nation to mark the event and the Queen received well over 100,000 messages of congratulation from all over the world. 30,000 jubilee medals were distributed and half a million 25-pence jubilee coins were issued. Those cast in silver have increased in value to around £15–£20 today, while those in copper-nickel languish at around the 50p mark.

The Silver Jubilee Medal, issued by the Royal Mint, shows the head of the Queen wearing St Edward's Crown, while on the reverse are the words 'The 25th Year of the Reign of Queen Elizabeth II 6 February 1977'. The Canadian version has the word 'Canada' at the top of the reverse with a maple leaf and '1952–1977', with the Royal Cypher below. The medal ribbon is white with a Garter blue centre with a narrow red stripe and red edges.

The Queen's Golden Jubilee in 2002 was tinged with sadness as both her mother and her sister died within seven weeks of each other.

On the day of Her Majesty's Golden Jubilee (6 February 2002), she became the oldest Monarch to have spent 50 years on the throne and she and the Duke of Edinburgh travelled more than 30,000 miles throughout the United Kingdom and overseas. The Queen visited 70 cities and towns in England, Scotland, Wales and Northern Ireland, using the Royal Train, the Royal Barge, the Gold State Coach, helicopters and aircraft – and her new Bentley.

A 'Party at the Palace' concert was held in the gardens of Buckingham Palace and was seen by a worldwide television audience exceeding 200 million.

On 4 June, a spectacular parade in The Mall involved 20,000 people with over a million watching.

688 men and women born on Accession Day (6 February 1952) attended the first themed Jubilee Garden Party at Buckingham Palace on 9 July and the Queen received over 17,000 congratulatory messages from all over the world.

All members of the armed forces with five years' service were awarded the Golden Jubilee Medal, with 366,000 medals being awarded costing £7.8 million.

## Keeper of the Privy Purse

The Privy Purse is the name given to the financial affairs of the Sovereign, and the Keeper is the man responsible for the management of the Queen's income from the Duchy of Lancaster (see Duchy of Lancaster) which funds her semi-official expenditure.

Apart from the Queen, the Keeper of the Privy Purse is the only person in the world who knows the full extent of Her Majesty's wealth. So while her bankers, Coutts & Co, know how much money she has in her account with them, they do not know if she has accounts at other banks, or the extent of her other holdings. The Keeper, who is Treasurer to Her Majesty, has to know everything in order to be able to advise her accordingly and to guide her in her financial affairs. In other words, he controls the royal cheque book.

The Keeper is a qualified accountant and an expert in financial management. A large team of around 46 men and women supports him, with a further 73 in the adjoining Finance and Property Office. Not only do they control the affairs of the Queen but organise the pensions of the Household and the salaries and wages of every member of the staff. They even look after the supply of stationery throughout the Palace, making sure there is a quantity of black-edged writing paper and envelopes in case there is a royal death.

The Queen, through the Keeper, is registered for Value Added Tax and her accounts are maintained in immaculate order. Even the sale of game, fowl, milk and everything else that is produced by the royal estates is operated by the Keeper of the Privy Purse through the Royal Gardens Enterprise and no one bargains more keenly on behalf of his royal employer than the Keeper of the Privy Purse.

## The Privy Purse

There really is a Privy Purse. It is a handsome, embroidered wallet, made of silk, about 18in square and is carried by the Keeper at the coronation ceremony, after which he is allowed to keep it.

## Knighthoods

When the Queen invests a man with the honour of knighthood, she taps him on the shoulder with the sword that belonged to her father, King George VI. His Majesty carried it as an officer in the Scots Guards and invariably used it when he conferred a knighthood. But, contrary to popular belief, the Queen does not say the words, 'Arise, Sir Knight,' or anything else. That's just Hollywood romanticism.

There are various categories of knighthood; the most commonly awarded being the KBE (Knight of the British Empire) even though there hasn't been an Empire since India gained her independence in 1948. The KBE is awarded on the 'advice' of the Prime Minister of the day and the Queen can only refuse the honour if she feels there are sufficient grounds.

In recent times, the KBE has been thought to be awarded too easily on occasions and to people who in times past would never have been considered for the honour. Rock stars, radio disc jockeys and businessmen who have made substantial political contributions have all been made knights, without any particular reference to good works, which in the past might have been contributory factors in their nomination.

Of course, there is nothing new in political contributors being rewarded with titles. In the early days of the 20th century, the then Prime Minister, David Lloyd George, was notorious for openly 'selling' knighthoods and peerages for large cash sums.

The most highly prized knighthood is the KCVO (Knight Commander of the Royal Victorian Order), because the award is solely in the gift of the Sovereign, without reference to, or 'advice' from, anyone. The KCVO is given for personal services to the Queen or to a member of her family. Queen Victoria instituted the Order on 21 April 1896 with the first recipient being her eldest son (later King Edward VII). Ladies weren't admitted until 1936 when Queen Mary became the first Dame Grand Cross.

You don't have to be British to become a Knight – or a Dame – but when honorary titles are conferred on foreigners, such as the late Douglas Fairbanks Jnr and Dr Henry Kissinger, they are not expected to use the style 'Sir'.

Douglas Fairbanks, though, admitted he sometimes used it to obtain the best tables in a restaurant.

Non-British ladies are similarly not allowed to call themselves Dame.

When one is being considered for knighthood (but not the KCVO), a letter is sent from the Prime Minister's office at 10 Downing Street informing the would-be recipient that the PM is considering forwarding his name to Her Majesty for the honour, but not making a definite offer. The person concerned has to reply by return, accepting or declining, though the days when the occasional gentleman asked to be excused on the grounds that he did not consider himself to be a suitable candidate are long gone.

Once the recipient has accepted, he is warned not to reveal the news to anyone, and there have been several occasions when an indiscreet remark from an excited soon-to-be Sir has led to a name being removed from the list. And it is rarely reinstated. However, one candidate, a former Lord Mayor of a major city, who even had his new stationery printed with his title on it, was informed that he was no longer being considered. Fortunately for him, the powers-that-be relented and the following year he finally got his 'K'.

# L

## Ladies-in-Waiting

The Queen has 14 Ladies-in-Waiting but they are not all on duty at the same time. The Mistress of the Robes, who is always a Duchess, heads them and her main duty is to attend Her Majesty in the robing room at the House of Lords prior to the State Opening of Parliament.

At one time, Ladies-in-Waiting were selected on the 'advice' of the Prime Minister; today there is no such pressure and the Queen chooses all her 'Ladies' herself. They are all friends and one, Lady Susan Hussey, was even invited to become Godmother to Prince William.

### The Queen's Ladies-in-Waiting

| | |
|---|---|
| *Mistress of the Robes* | The Duchess of Grafton |
| *Ladies* | The Countess of Airlie Diana |
| | Lady Farnham |
| | The Hon. Mary Morrison |
| | The Lady Susan Hussey |
| | The Lady Elton |
| | Mrs Michael Gordon Lennox |
| | The Hon. Mrs Whitehead |
| | Mrs Robert de Pass |

The Queen is attended by six permanent 'Ladies' and several 'Extras' none of whom is required any longer to assist Her Majesty to dress and undress in her bedroom as they did in days gone by. These days, the 'Ladies', who are unpaid but with expenses reimbursed, work a fortnight at a time, accompanying the Queen on mainly informal occasions. They have their own sitting room and office at Buckingham Palace, where they also reply, on the Queen's behalf, to letters from the public (every letter to Her Majesty receives an acknowledgement).

The 'Ladies', of whom most have known the Queen for many years, come from upper-class backgrounds and during engagements their duties include mingling with guests and putting them at ease before they meet Her Majesty. Other duties include any personal shopping the Queen requires and, as one of the 'Women' put it, the ability to stand for hours without food or drink and occasionally to possess a bladder with a tank-like capacity. Their good humour is a byword in Palace circles as is their ability to mix with people from all walks of life and from every station.

When they accompany the Queen on social occasions, they are treated, according to them, with disparaging condescension, or, occasionally, with near adulation because of their nearness to the Sovereign. And they all say the main question they are asked when they accompany Her Majesty on a visit is, 'What if she needs to go to the lavatory?' The answer is that a 'retiring room' should be made available for her exclusive use.

## Likes and Dislikes

Newcomers to the Royal Household are quickly made aware of the likes and dislikes of members of the Royal Family, and they soon realise, the faster they learn, the better it is for them.

The Queen does not care to see her staff, apart from liveried servants, in three-piece suits, so waistcoats are out. She also prefers men in dark suits to brown, adopting the old adage that 'gentlemen do not wear brown in town'. Black lace-up shoes are better than loafers and the cardinal sin in royal eyes is to see someone at a formal function wearing a made-up bow tie. It is said Her Majesty can spot one at 20 paces and Palace officials, if they do not already know how, quickly learn to tie their own bows.

Only the Household and staff use napkin rings in royal residences. The Queen and her family do not need them because there is a fresh napkin at every meal. King George V was once highly amused to find one at his place when he dined with friends, remarking, 'What's this? It's far too big for my finger.'

The Queen hates anyone trying to pet her dogs. They respond to her and only her. There is no dogs' cemetery at any of the royal residences; instead, the animals are buried at various spots on the Sandringham Estate, usually near a favourite tree, with a small stone to mark the grave.

Her Majesty likes to drink water, but it must be still and not sparkling, and preferably Malvern, bottles of which accompany her on every tour. She has a vast collection of vintage champagnes in the royal cellars, but she does not care for the drink and even when drinking a toast she will usually just wet her lips to be polite.

The Princess Royal does not drink any alcohol. At State Banquets, the wine steward places orange juice or Coke in front of her.

The Queen does not take sugar in her tea, but she carries her own sweetener, which she adds herself.

When the Queen needs to see a doctor, optician or hairdresser, they come to her, not the other way around. The only occasion when she goes out to see a medical consultant is when she visits her dentist (who is a part-time member of the Royal Household with the ancient title of Surgeon-Dentist) in Harley Street, because he has all the necessary equipment on hand. A qualified pedicurist looks after the royal feet, cutting Her Majesty's toenails in the privacy of her own bedroom.

Prince Philip has a fully equipped barber's chair above his private apartments in Buckingham Palace and a hairdresser comes in once a week to give the royal locks a trim.

Both the Queen and Prince Philip dislike long, rambling speeches, so when they are to attend a function where speeches are planned, the organisers are warned that no speech should exceed 12 minutes.

If the royal couple are going to the theatre (a rare occasions these days), they will have a light supper before leaving. It is usually something like smoked salmon and scrambled eggs.

Her Majesty enjoys doing crosswords, but refuses to use a thesaurus, saying it is cheating.

The Queen calls all her personal staff by their Christian names – even her flower arranger Mrs Pentney is addressed as Pat – and if Paul Wybrew, Her Majesty's long-serving Page, was called anything but Paul, he would think he had done something very wrong.

Thirteen people are not permitted to sit down to luncheon or dinner. It is not because the Queen is particularly superstitious (though she does throw salt over her shoulder) it is because she feels some of her guests may be.

Her Majesty prefers woollen blankets and linen sheets to duvets and her sheets are six inches longer than those of Prince Philip as she likes a longer 'turn-back'. She also prefers the radio to television, with BBC Radio Four said to be her favourite station. She has a Roberts radio on her bedside table at all her residences.

The only time she watches television is when she is alone in the evening and if there is racing on, her favourite sport (see Racing). If one of her horses has been running and she has been unable to watch the race, a recording is sent to the Palace immediately.

The Princess Royal hates to be driven and insists on taking the wheel herself on practically all occasions. Her personal protection officers all know this and (reluctantly) obey. They are soon made aware of her likes and dislikes. They know she doesn't care for small talk and that they must make sure CDs of her favourite music are available in the Bentley before they set off. She is not a great fan of classical music. Food is a necessary evil in her view. She eats like a sparrow and one of her staff said, if she could take a pill instead of food, she would. However, she enjoys small, intimate dinner parties and guests at Gatcombe Park say she is a brilliant hostess.

The Queen has never rung a doorbell in her life, or knocked on a door. Whenever she is due somewhere on a private visit, her police officer will telephone from his mobile when they are a few minutes away, and the hosts arc always waiting for her on the doorstep.

Tennis is not on the list of Royal favourite sports. The Queen has visited Wimbledon only twice during her reign, in 1977 and 2010, the earlier occasion being when she presented the Women's Singles Championship Shield to Virginia Wade. The Princess Royal is also not much of an enthusiast, saying that Wimbledon is too 'cauldron-like'.

The Duke of Kent is President of The All-England Club and always attends Wimbledon fortnight where he is a great favourite with the ball boys and girls.

Prince Charles will not travel without his own white, leather lavatory seat.

## Lily Font

The Lily Font, so named because of its lily-shaped stem, has been used for all royal christenings since the baptism of Queen Victoria's first child, Victoria, the Princess Royal, in 1841. The font is 17in high and 16½in in diameter and made of silver gilt. It bears the royal arms of Queen Victoria and the joint arms of Victoria and Albert.

It was used at the baptism of all the Queen's children and grandchildren with the exception of Princess Beatrice who was baptised at Sandringham (see Christenings and Godparents). The Lily Font used to be kept at Windsor Castle, but it is now housed, with the Crown Jewels, at the Tower of London.

## Liveries

All male domestic staff are required to wear livery when on duty. The present outfits date from 1967. Prior to this, they wore the battledress tunics introduced during the Second World War.

Footmen wear a black tailcoat and trousers with a soft white shirt with a turndown collar, black tie and scarlet waistcoat.

On semi-State occasions, footmen wear a scarlet tailcoat, white stiff shirt (which they say is very uncomfortable) and bow tie. For full State functions such as State Banquets, they wear scarlet livery decorated with gold braid, scarlet plush knee breeches, pink stockings and black buckle shoes.

Some of this livery is well over 70 years old and, as the cost to replace it today would be over £2,000, some of the outfits have been worn by generations of royal servants. One of the qualifications when one is applying for a job as footman is that one should be able to fit the State livery – not the other way around.

Pages, who are senior members of the domestic Household, wear three different outfits. Normal daily dress is a blue Household coat with black trousers, soft white shirt, black tie and blue waistcoat with gilt buttons. On semi-State occasions, the only difference from their normal daily outfit is that they wear a stiff shirt with winged collar, white bow tie and white waistcoat. For the most important State occasions, Pages wear dark-blue livery with gold braid, white wool, cloth breeches, stockings and black, buckled shoes.

The livery for those staff employed in the Royal Mews is very similar to that used for the past 200 years, only the royal cypher changes with each successive sovereign.

Coachmen, postilions and outriders, have four different liveries known as Plain, Ascot, Full State and Semi-State. Coachmen wear cream breeches, black jacket and black top hat in plain rig for everyday use; scarlet tunic with gold-laced top hat during the Royal Procession at Ascot; and the same outfit but with a tricorn hat and wig for full State occasions such as the State Opening of Parliament. Postilions and outriders wear similar outfits but at Ascot they also wear a cap and wig.

## Lords and Baronesses-in-Waiting

The Lords or Baronesses-in-Waiting who are working members of the House of Lords are appointed to the Royal Household on the advice of the Prime Minister from among the Government Whips in the House of Lords. Consequently, they change with each Government. Their Household duties include representing Her Majesty at funerals or memorial services and meeting, on behalf of the Queen, important visitors arriving in or departing from the United Kingdom.

The other Lords and Baronesses are non-political and are appointed by the Sovereign.

| *Lords and Baronesses-in-Waiting* | The Earl of Airlie (Permanent) |
| | The Lord Camoys (Permanent) |
| | The Lord Luce (Permanent) |
| | The Lord Janvrin (Permanent) |
| | The Viscount Brookeborough |
| | The Viscount Hood |
| | The Baroness Farringdon of Ribbleton |
| | The Baroness Thornton |
| | The Lord Tunnicliffe |
| | Lord Faulkner of Worcester |
| *Extras* | The Lord Denham |
| | The Lord Strabolgi |
| | The Lord St John of Bletso |
| | The Baroness Trumpington |
| | The Baroness Seccombe |
| | The Lord Tordoff |

## Lord Great Chamberlain

One of the Great Officers of State – not to be confused with the Lord Chamberlain – the Lord Great Chamberlain is responsible for royal matters in the Palace of Westminster, where his office is located in the House of Lords. Three families hold the right to the title: the Marquesate of Cholmondeley (pronounced Chumley), the Earldom of Ancaster and the Marquesate of Lincolnshire, with each family holding it for the duration of a reign. The present Lord Great Chamberlain is the seventh Marquess of Cholmondeley, who, at the State Opening of Parliament, symbolically offers to Her Majesty the gold key of the Palace, which she then returns after briefly touching it.

## Lord High Admiral

The Queen is Lord High Admiral of the Royal Navy, a post that originated in the 14th century, and continued for nearly 300 years to be held by a succession of naval officers and later aristocrats. But it was with the restoration of the Monarchy in 1660 that Charles II conferred the title on his brother the Duke of York (later James II). It then lapsed until it was revived in 1827 for the Duke of Clarence (later William IV), Queen Victoria's uncle. He resigned the post a year later and it wasn't until 1 April 1964 that the Admiralty persuaded Her Majesty to accept the title.

She is also the first and, so far, only woman to have held the post. She has a special Lord High Admiral's flag that is flown when Her Majesty is at sea, and at naval establishments ashore on official occasions, when it flies alongside the Royal Standard.

## Lord High Commissioner

The Lord High Commissioner is appointed by the Queen to represent her at the annual General Assembly of the Church of Scotland in Edinburgh. This normally takes place during May when the Lord High Commissioner resides in the Palace of

Holyroodhouse in great splendour, taking precedence over all others, including members of the Royal Family, except the Sovereign, the Duke of Edinburgh and the Duke of Rothesay (the Prince of Wales).

The week is marked by luncheons, dinners, receptions and garden parties, a State Banquet and the colourful ceremony of the keys when a full guard of honour attends the Lord High Commissioner.

The office is usually held for two consecutive years, but can be limited to a single appointment at Her Majesty's command.

In 2007, Prince Andrew, Duke of York, was appointed Lord High Commissioner, attending the opening and closing ceremonies of the General Assembly.

## Lord Lieutenants

Every county in England and Wales has a Lord Lieutenant, who can be female, but they are still called Lord rather than Lady Lieutenant. The post was established by Henry VIII to represent the Crown in local military matters. Today, they no longer perform the same function, being responsible mainly for the organisation of royal visits to their county. Whenever a member of the Royal Family arrives, the Lord Lieutenant, or the Vice-Lieutenant or Deputy Lieutenant, is there to greet them and accompany them for the duration of the visit.

The Queen appoints the Lord Lieutenant on the advice of the Prime Minister but they do not have to be peers or knights. Among their other duties is recommending men and women to become Justices of the Peace (JPs) and they are required to retire on reaching the age of 75.

At one time, all holders of the post were either ex-military or naval officers, but this no longer applies. And neither do they wear the full-dress uniform of scarlet tunic and cocked hat, complete with sword. Today, they wear a navy-blue uniform, with scarlet stripes on the trousers (ladies wear skirts) and a scarlet band around a military-style peaked cap.

To be a Lord Lieutenant remains one of the most prestigious

positions in the country and the people who have been appointed need to be gregarious, good with people from all walks of life – and, on occasions, have a good sense of humour and a thick skin!

## Lord of Man

The Queen is Lord of Man, a title held by the British sovereign since the 18th century, when George III first held it in 1765. The Government of that day bought the Isle of Man from the Duke of Athol, whose family had inherited it from the Earls of Derby, who, in turn, had held it for 300 years.

Just as the Queen is known as the Duke of Lancaster in that county, so on the Isle of Man she is toasted as 'The Queen – Lord of Man', not 'Lady'.

## Lord of the Isles

Prince Charles is Lord of the Isles, a title he holds automatically as Heir Apparent to the throne of Scotland. The Clan Macdonald held the title originally, until James V of Scotland seized it for the Crown in 1540. It has remained in the possession of the Sovereign ever since.

## Lord Steward

The Lord Steward (as opposed to the Lord High Steward, which is a temporary appointment, made usually only for Coronations) is one of the three Great Officers of the Royal Household. Until the 1920s, this was a political appointment changing with each new Government.

Since then it has been non-political, with the Lord Steward being the titular head of the Master of the Household's Department but, again, this is a part-time appointment with his attendance required at Buckingham Palace only on all important State occasions when his task is to present guests to Her Majesty and His Royal Highness.

## Loyal Toast

There is often some confusion about the correct way to offer the loyal toast, and to whom it should be drunk.

### Offering the Loyal Toast

On formal occasions, the procedure is as follows:

The toastmaster calls for silence, everyone stands, the first verse of the National Anthem is sung, the speaker then calls for the toast with the words, 'Her Majesty, The Queen,' the toast is drunk and everyone then sits down.

If further toasts are proposed, the order is: The Duke of Edinburgh, followed by the Prince of Wales (if it is in Scotland, it will be the Duke of Rothesay), then would follow the other members of the Royal Family, if required, in order of precedence.

Loyal toasts drunk in the Royal Navy are offered sitting down.

The origin of the seated toast on board a ship is said to date from a dinner when the Duke of Clarence (later William IV) hit his head on rising and declared that in future all loyal toasts aboard ship should be from a sitting position. One of the few exceptions to this rule was in the former Royal Yacht, *Britannia*, where the loyal toast was always drunk with the officers standing. Nobody seems to know why.

## Lying-in-State

When the Sovereign dies, it is usual for the body to lie in State for a period so that members of the Royal Family, important foreign dignitaries and the general public may pay their respects.

The duration of the Lying-in-State can vary, with each Sovereign deciding beforehand the length and venue. It was King Edward VII who laid down the plans for his own Lying-in-State and which have been followed by his successors.

Both King George V and George VI died at Sandringham and the Royal Train brought their coffins to London, from where they were taken, in procession, to St Stephen's Hall in the Palace of Westminster and placed on a purple-draped catafalque. Four Gentlemen at Arms and four officers of the Brigade of Guards stood silently, with heads bowed over their arms reversed, with colleagues relieving them in relays 24 hours a day.

King George V lay in state for four days; his son, King George VI, for three.

The public have been admitted since the days of King Edward VII, when a quarter-of-a-million of his subjects passed the catafalque in silent tribute. By the time of the Lying-in-State of George V and George VI, the number had risen to around a million.

The most dramatic climax to a Lying-in-State occurred when on the final night of the ceremony in honour of King George V. His eldest son, and new King, Edward VIII, decided that he and his three brothers, the Dukes of York, Gloucester and Kent, would stand guard over their father's coffin. In full dress uniform, they stood around the bier for 20 minutes, with heads bowed, between the officers already mounting the vigil.

Of course, when Edward VIII died in 1972, he was no longer King, but Duke of Windsor, and no official Lying-in-State was possible at Westminster, but on the orders of the Queen, his body was brought to St George's Chapel at Windsor, where it lay in State for two days, before the interment in the Royal Burial Ground at Frogmore.

Four officers of the Household Division maintained watch on the catafalque and thousands of people filed past to pay their respects to their former Sovereign. Her Majesty also commanded that the flag that flies night and day on the Round Tower of Windsor Castle should be lowered to half-mast until the day of the funeral and all flags in the town of Windsor followed suit.

## Maids of Honour

At the Queen's coronation, six Maids of Honour, all unmarried as the title implies, attended Her Majesty. They were:

Lady Jane Vane-Tempest-Stewart
Lady Rosemary Spencer-Churchill
Lady Mary Baillie-Hamilton
Lady Moyra Hamilton
Lady Jane Heathcote-Drummond-Willoughby
Lady Anne Coke

## Marriages

Two important statutes govern the marriages of members of the Royal Family. The first is the Act of Settlement, 1701, which states that no Roman Catholic or anyone married to a Catholic may succeed to the throne. So, when Prince Michael of Kent married a Catholic, Marie-Christine von Reibnitz, in 1978, he had to renounce his place in the Line of Succession. (Not that there was ever much chance of him becoming king anyway.) However, his children, who are Anglicans, are still in the Line.

It was also thought that one of the reasons why the Prince of Wales could not marry Camilla Parker Bowles was that she was a Roman Catholic. But that was not true. Camilla is not, and never has been a Catholic. Her former husband, Andrew Parker Bowles, is a Catholic and they were married in a Catholic service at the Guards Chapel, but Camilla was not required to convert to Catholicism, only to agree that their children would be baptised in the Catholic faith.

The other statute is the Royal Marriages Act, 1772, which requires that all lineal descendents of George II must first obtain the consent of the Sovereign before a marriage can be valid. The idea was to prevent anyone 'unsuitable' marrying into the Royal Family. There is, however, a get-out clause. If the Sovereign refuses to give consent, a member of the Royal Family, once they have reached the age of 25, may signify to the Privy Council an intention to marry and then both Houses of Parliament have 12 months to object. If they do not disapprove, the marriage is then lawful.

The most celebrated recent case when this could have taken place was in 1955 when Princess Margaret had fallen in love with a divorced man, Group Captain Peter Townsend. In those days, such a marriage could not have received the consent of the Queen, so they would have had to have had a civil ceremony and the Princess would have been required to give up her place in the Line of Succession.

However, after careful consideration, she decided not to proceed, issuing a statement that included the words '...mindful of the Church's teaching that Christian marriage is indissoluble...I have decided to put these considerations before any other.' Princess Margaret's 18-year marriage to the Earl of Snowdon ended in divorce in 1978.

## Master of the Household

The Master of the Household runs the largest department by far in the Royal Household with several hundred staff working under his supervision. He is the 'Hotel Manager' of the Palace, looking after all the domestic arrangements of the Royal Family and the Household.

All the men (no female has ever held the post) who have become Master are retired senior officers in the Army, Royal Navy and Royal Air Force. They are chosen because attention to detail was paramount in their former careers and that is what is required here.

Two Deputies support the Master with one acting as Permanent Equerry to the Queen and organising all her private domestic arrangements. The other looks after 'F' 'G' and 'H' branches, standing for Food, General and Housekeeping. There is also a 'C' branch based at Windsor, with the 'C' standing for Craftsmen.

The Master of the Household organises the kitchen which can serve up to 600 meals a day, the State Banquets, the ladies who vacuum the Royal carpets, the footmen who open the door to visitors to the Palace and the two men who wind and maintain the 300 clocks all year round. If the Queen needs new pillows for her bed, the Master provides them, with the money coming from the Keeper of the Privy Purse. The pillows would come under 'H' branch, while any curtains or carpets would come under 'G'.

'General' also controls the footmen, butlers and under-butlers and pages; in other words, those who come into contact with visitors as well as the Royal Family. In a hotel they would be called 'front of house'. They are the image that is presented to the outside world; the Master of the Household is their boss and they all know he has only one standard – perfection.

## Maundy Services

On the Thursday of Holy Week, the Queen distributes money to a number of men and women at a cathedral either in London or elsewhere in the United Kingdom. It is the service of the Royal Maundy that is so old no record exists of when it actually began, though the ceremony is based on the Last Supper when Christ washed the feet of his disciples. What is evident is that Edward the Confessor, one of the most pious of all English Monarchs, used the occasion to humble himself by kneeling and washing the feet of the poor and then giving them alms. When you consider what the state of these poor unfortunates must have been in those days, it says much for the King's sense of duty that he could bring himself even to touch them.

The ceremony continued for centuries, with different sovereigns making significant changes to the routine. Elizabeth I did wash the feet of the poor, but only after her courtiers had first bathed the recipients to make sure their bodies would not cause regal offence.

Charles II attended the service in Whitehall in 1667, but left the washing of the feet to the Bishop of London, while in 1685, James II not only washed the feet of 52 men and women, but also kissed them.

For two centuries, the custom of the Sovereign attending in person was abandoned, only to be revived in 1932 when King George V went to Westminster Abbey, where the service was traditionally held, and distributed the Maundy Money that had replaced the gifts of food and drink, and the washing of the feet had also long been discontinued, but the practice remains of those attending the Sovereign wearing white linen cloths as a reminder of those days when the feet were washed. Nosegays of herbs are also carried, as they were when they were required as a safeguard against infection.

Two purses, one red and the other white, contain £5.50 in cash in the red purse and the specially minted silver Maundy coins, one for each year of the Sovereign's life, in the white. Yeomen of the Guard carry them on dishes in full dress Tudor uniform, and being poor is no longer a requirement to be a recipient.

Instead, recipients are nominated by the clergy of the parish in recognition of their good works over the years. Maundy Money occasionally comes up for sale at prices beyond its intrinsic value. But most recipients keep their Maundy Money for the rest of their lives as a reminder of the part they played in one of the most historic and religious ceremonies in royal pageantry.

## Medical Household

The Royal Family and members of the Household are able to call on the services of some of the most eminent medical practitioners in the country. They are known as the Medical Household which consists of two Physicians to the Queen, the senior being the Head of the Medical Household, and the other being a homeopath (the Queen is a firm believer in this form of medicine), as well as other professional appointees: a sergeant-surgeon; a surgeon gynaecologist; a surgeon-dentist; an orthopaedic surgeon; and a surgeon-oculist. There is also a coroner and apothecaries in London, Windsor and Sandringham.

Those at Buckingham Palace and Windsor Castle are salaried and hold daily surgeries for members of the Household, while the senior members of the Medical Household are paid an honorarium.

In Scotland, there are two physicians and two surgeons, two extra surgeons and two apothecaries to the Household at Balmoral and the Palace of Holyroodhouse.

In addition, there are several honorary appointments, which, though technically not part of the Medical Household, serve when required at functions such as State Banquets, Investitures and Garden Parties. These come from a branch of the armed forces and are designated as Queen's Honorary Physicians (QHP), Surgeons (QHS), Dental Surgeons (QHDS) and Nurses (QHNS).

## The Royal Mews

Whenever the Queen travels by road, whether it is by carriage, on horseback or by motorcar, all the arrangements are the responsibility of the Crown Equerry. He is the man who runs the Royal Mews on a day-to-day basis, even though the titular head is the Master of the Horse, third in order of precedence at Court. However, although he can be seen riding immediately behind the Queen in State processions, his duties are mainly ceremonial and do not involve him in the operation of the Mews.

There are Royal Mews at all royal residences, with the one at Buckingham Palace receiving the most attention as most of the official functions start and end here. The Mews at Buckingham Palace dates from 1825, when George IV ordered John Nash (who also designed Regent Street) to build a property suitable for his horses and carriages. The Mews are constructed around a quadrangle with the east side reserved for the State coaches and carriages, with the horses stabled in the north and west sides. The royal cars and limousines are also garaged within the Mews and there is a friendly rivalry between those who look after the horses and those who prefer their horsepower under the bonnet of a powerful vehicle.

The staff live in apartments above the coach houses and the entire Mews has a village-like atmosphere, completely separate from those who live and work in the Palace proper.

## The State Coaches

### The Gold State Coach
24 ft long, 8ft 3in wide and 12ft high; used for every coronation since that of George IV; built in 1762 for George III, who rode in it for the first time to the State Opening of Parliament the day after it was delivered; gilded all over and decorated with panels painted by Giovanni Battista Cipriani, the celebrated, 18th-century Florentine artist; the harness is made of rich, red morocco leather and the coachman's footboard is in the shape of a large scallop shell.

### The Irish State Coach
Named after the builder, who was also Lord Mayor of Dublin; bought for Queen Victoria in 1852, but the one now used is not the original; much lighter than the Gold State Coach, with black-painted panels adorned in gold with the Royal Coat of Arms and the insignia of the Order of the Garter; used by the Queen each November as she is driven to the Palace of Westminster for the State Opening of Parliament.

### The Scottish State Coach
Occupies third place in the carriage hierarchy of the Mews; the crown of Scotland is mounted on the roof with the Royal Arms

of Scotland and the insignia of the Order of the Thistle on the sides; the Queen uses the coach for all State occasions held in Scotland, but also occasionally in England; the Royal Family love riding in it because it is by far the most comfortable of all the State Coaches; it is also the most elegant, with its glass-panelled roof and large side windows so the interior lighting is superb. Originally built in 1830, Her Majesty commissioned an Edinburgh company to completely refurbish the coach in 1969.

### Queen Alexandra's State Coach

So named because it was originally used by Her Majesty who continued to make use of it after the death of her husband, King Edward VII. Newly-appointed Ambassadors who wish to present their credentials to the Queen at Buckingham Palace, they are driven from their official residence to the Palace in this coach; it is also seen every year at the State Opening of Parliament when it carries the Imperial State Crown guarded by the Comptroller of the Lord Chamberlain's Office; the attendants are invariably the Queen's Bargemaster and one Waterman, a tradition that dates from the days when the crown was transported from the Tower of London to the Palace of Westminster via the River Thames.

### The Glass Coach

This was the carriage in which Lady Diana Spencer travelled to St Paul's Cathedral for her marriage to the Prince of Wales in 1981; it was built in 1881, for the then Lord Mayor of London, and was bought by King George V for his coronation in 1911; since then it has been used for nearly every royal wedding, including that of Princess Elizabeth and the Duke of Edinburgh in 1947; a very popular coach with the public because the large picture windows enable the spectators to see who is inside.

### The 1902 State Landau

Following the wedding service of the Prince and Princess of Wales, the couple were driven back to Buckingham Palace in the Landau; it was built in 1902, the second year of King Edward VII's reign, and is usually seen in an open format, though it can be closed if the weather dictates; the upholstery is of rich, satin crimson, with plenty of gold leaf decorating the exterior. Six postilion horses normally draw the 1902 State Landau.

## Military Knights of Windsor

These are all retired former Army officers who are appointed by the Queen, with their main duties being to attend St George's Chapel every Sunday to pray for the Sovereign and the Knights of the Garter, to whom they are attached.

Called 'Poor Knights' in the 15th century, after Edward III founded them in 1348 (at the same time as he founded the Order of the Garter), their title was changed after much lobbying of King William IV in 1833, to their present style.

There are 26 Knights – who are not, in fact, allowed to style themselves 'Sir' – and one of their privileges is to lead the procession to St George's Chapel for the annual Garter Service, wearing their uniforms of blue trousers, scarlet, frock-tailed coat and cocked hat.

The Knights live in a terraced row of houses immediately inside the castle walls, opposite St George's Chapel.

### The Garter Prayer

Said by the Military Knights every Sunday:
'God save our Gracious Sovereign and all the Companions, living and departed, of the Most Honourable and Noble Order of the Garter.'

## Names

The surname of the Royal Family is Windsor. The Queen's grandfather, King George V, adopted it in 1917 during the First World War owing to the anti-German sentiment that was prevalent throughout the British Empire at the time. Prior to this, the surname of the Royal Family was Saxe-Coburg-Gotha and, at the time, when His Majesty ordered the name change, he also told his close relations, who also bore German names, to change theirs to more British-sounding surnames.

His Serene Highness Prince Louis of Battenberg assumed the surname Mountbatten and was created Marquess of Milford Haven. His elder son, George Battenberg, was given the courtesy title of Earl of Medina, while the younger Battenberg son, another Louis, became Lord Louis Mountbatten, a title he bore until he was created Viscount Mountbatten of Burma in 1946 and Earl Mountbatten of Burma the following year. Another of the Battenbergs, Prince Alexander, who fought as a Captain in the Grenadier Guards, was created Marquess of Carisbrooke.

The King's wife, Queen Mary, (who had been Princess Mary of Teck) had two surviving brothers, both serving in the British Army and they, too, relinquished their German titles and surnames, assuming the name Cambridge after their maternal grandmother's family. The Duke of Teck became Marquess of Cambridge despite petitioning the King to make him a British duke. He was refused because the rank was reserved for His Majesty's own sons who would become Dukes of Cornwall (later Windsor after the abdication), York, Gloucester and Kent. The Marquess of Cambridge's younger brother, Prince Alexander, became Earl of Athlone.

So, all German-sounding names and titles in the Royal Family were swept away in a single gesture and replaced with Windsor, Carisbrooke, Cambridge, Milford Haven and Athlone. Nothing could have been more British and, in all fairness, those German princes and dukes were all serving in the British armed forces and their patriotism had never been in doubt.

When Prince Philip of Greece married Princess Elizabeth in 1947, after he had served in the Royal Navy during the Second World War, he, too, renounced his Greek titles and assumed the surname Mountbatten. And when their daughter, Princess Anne (now the Princess Royal) married Mark Phillips in 1973, she signed the wedding certificate Mountbatten-Windsor in tribute to her father's name.

## Nannies and Nursemaids

For generations, royal nannies have been a law unto themselves. They see more of their royal charges than their parents, and they frequently become surrogate mothers.

Prince Charles had two nannies – Helen Lightbody and Mabel Anderson – on whom he depended so much that when the time came for him to go away to school, it wasn't his mother he cried for but his nannies.

The Queen had a famous nanny, Miss Margaret 'Bobo' McDonald, the only royal servant who was permitted to call her by her pet name, 'Lillibet'. And when Miss McDonald retired, she remained living in a suite of rooms immediately above the Queen's private apartments at Buckingham Palace where Her Majesty visited her every day until she died.

The nannies and nursemaids did not have to eat with the other staff in the Servant's Hall, neither did they make their own beds or clean their own shoes. Other servants did all this for them.

The nannies and nursemaids taught the children in their charge good manners from the earliest age. When Prince William and Prince Harry were taken to see their grandmother, the Queen, by their nursemaid or nanny, they learnt to bow as soon as they could walk. The nanny also taught them the order of precedence so that when the Queen's grandchildren were presented to her it was in the order of their place in the line of succession with William and Harry first, followed by the others.

Because of the Royal Family's reliance on their nannies and nursemaids, the relationship often lasted long after the servants' usefulness had been outlived, with most of them being looked after for the remainder of their lives.

## National Anthem

England was the first country in the world to adopt the practice of having a particular tune as its national anthem. It all began over 260 years ago, when the patriotic song, 'For Two Voices' including the line 'God save the King . . .' was first publicly performed in London in 1745.

It took place at the Theatre Royal, Drury Lane, when the leader of the orchestra, Thomas Arne, felt there was need for such a rallying song following the defeat of the King's armies by the rebellious Bonnie Prince Charlie. Arne made a special arrangement of the song, supposedly written by John Simpson a year earlier after a proclamation in Edinburgh that Charles Stewart was to be king of both Scotland and England, seizing the crown from George II. The tune proved to be an immediate success with the audience and was repeated night after night.

A few nights later, a former pupil of Thomas Arne, Charles Burney, produced a similar arrangement of the same song, which was sung at Covent Garden Theatre. So began what became the custom of singing and playing the tune that has been adopted as the national anthem at the end of every theatre performance in the land. That custom has now died out in practically every theatre and cinema.

The tune was later extended to become a loyal greeting whenever the Sovereign made a public appearance, and many people believe that the introduction of the National Anthem was a turning point in England's history. For shortly after it was first played, the English Army, under Marshal Wade, stemmed the tide of rebellion and defeated the Scottish Army in 1746 at the Battle of Culloden.

There have been many claimants to the original copyright of the work, but no one has fully established ownership, even John Simpson, who turned out to be not the composer, but merely the publisher.

If anyone could prove legal right to the ownership they would become multi-millionaires, as the royalties – it was this tune that gave birth to the use of the word to signify payment for the right to sing or play a melody – would be worth more than any other single tune in history. It is the 'Bible' of the musical world.

Back in the 18th century, the immediate success of 'God Save the King' soon found its way around the world with countries such as Denmark, Sweden, Switzerland, Russia, Liechtenstein and later the United States, all using the tune as a setting for their own words.

After two-and-a-half centuries, it remains the most popular anthem in the world and the most frequently sung.

### The Standard Version of 'God Save the Queen'

(The first and third verses are the most commonly sung)

God save our gracious Queen,
Long live our noble Queen,
God save the Queen;
Send her victorious,
Happy and glorious,
Long to reign over us;
God save the Queen.

O Lord, our God, arise,
Scatter her enemies,
And make them fall.
Confound their politics,
Frustrate their knavish tricks,
On Thee our hopes we fix,
God save us all.

Thy choicest gifts in store,
On her be pleased to pour;
Long may she reign;
May she defend our laws,
And ever give us cause
To sing with heart and voice
God save the Queen.

The Isle of Man has its own anthem, while in Wales, 'Land of My Fathers' (usually sung in Welsh) is regarded as the National Anthem.

'Flower of Scotland' has been adopted as the national song north of the border, and is sung at rugby international matches, but it is not yet accepted as the National Anthem.

## Oath of Allegiance

The Oath of Allegiance to the Sovereign is taken by Members of Parliament of both Houses, Privy Councillors, ordained priests in the Church of England and those serving in the Army, Royal Navy and Royal Air Force. The Oath is also taken by those seeking to become naturalised British citizens.

The wording of the present oath is:
 'I [name given] do swear that I will be faithful and bear true allegiance to Her Majesty, Queen Elizabeth II, Her heirs and successors, according to law, so help me God.'

Some MPs, who are not supporters of the Monarchy, deliberately cross their fingers when taking the oath, to show they do not really mean it. But, unless they at least pretend to take the oath, they cannot become Members of Parliament – or collect their salaries and expenses.

## Olympic and Commonwealth Games

If the Olympic Games are held in Britain or one of the Commonwealth countries, it is usual to invite a member of the Royal Family to officially declare them open and to conduct the closing ceremony.

When the Games were held in London in 1948, the first Olympics after the conclusion of the Second World War, King George VI performed the opening ceremony. In 1956, the Games were staged in Melbourne, Australia, with the Duke of Edinburgh doing the honours and, in 1976 in Montreal, Her Majesty, as Queen of Canada, opened the Games. It was at these Games that Princess Anne competed as a member of the British Three-Day Event equestrian team, where she was concussed after a severe fall on the cross-country section, but she remounted her horse immediately and completed the event. Since retiring from competitive sport, the Princess has continued her involvement with the Olympic movement as President of the British Olympic Association, and she was an active member of the team that succeeded in winning the nomination of Britain to be host for the 2012 Olympic Games. Her Royal Highness is also President of Fédération Equestre Internationale (FEI).

The Princess's former husband, Mark Phillips, was also an Olympic competitor, having been a member of the United Kingdom Equestrian team that won the Gold Medal at the 1972 Games in Munich.

A member of the Royal Family always conducts the Opening and Closing ceremonies of the Commonwealth Games. During the Queen's reign, the full list is as follows:

| 1954 | Canada (Vancouver) | The Duke of Edinburgh closed the Games |
| 1958 | Wales (Cardiff) | The Duke of Edinburgh opened and closed the Games |
| 1962 | Australia (Perth) | The Duke of Edinburgh opened and closed the Games |
| 1966 | Jamaica (Kingston) | The Duke of Edinburgh opened and closed the Games |

| 1970 | Scotland (Edinburgh) | The Duke of Edinburgh opened the Games; the Queen closed the Games |
| 1974 | New Zealand (Christchurch) | The Duke of Edinburgh opened the Games; the Queen closed the Games |
| 1978 | Canada (Edmonton) | The Queen opened the Games; the Duke of Edinburgh closed the Games |
| 1982 | Australia (Brisbane) | The Duke of Edinburgh opened the Games; the Queen closed the Games |
| 1986 | Scotland (Edinburgh) | The Duke of Edinburgh opened the Games; the Queen closed the Games |
| 1990 | New Zealand (Auckland) | Prince Edward opened the Games; the Queen closed the Games |
| 1994 | Canada (Victoria) | The Queen opened the Games |
| 1998 | Malaysia (Kuala Lumpur) | The Earl of Wessex closed the Games |
| 2002 | England (Manchester) | The Queen opened and closed the Games |
| 2006 | Australia (Melbourne) | The Queen opened the Games; the Earl of Wessex closed the Games |
| 2010 | India (Delhi) | Prince Charles opened the Games |
| 2012 | Scotland (Glasgow) | Royal attendance has yet to be confirmed |

From 1954–66, the Games were known as the Empire and Commonwealth Games. From 1970–74, they were known as the British Commonwealth Games and, since 1978, they have been known as the Commonwealth Games.

## Order of Precedence and Order of Succession

The difference between the two orders is that spouses are included in the Order of Precedence but not in the Order of Succession to the Throne.

### The Current Order of Precedence at Court in Britain

The Queen
The Duke of Edinburgh
The Prince of Wales
The Duchess of Cornwall [only when accompanying her husband]
Prince William of Wales
Prince Henry of Wales
The Duke of York
Princess Beatrice
Princess Eugenie
The Earl of Wessex
The Countess of Wessex
Viscount Severn
Lady Louise Windsor
The Princess Royal
Peter Phillips
Zara Phillips
Viscount Linley
Lady Sarah Chatto
Followed by the Gloucesters and Kents

## Order of Precedence for Ladies at Court

At the time of the marriage of the Prince of Wales and the Duchess of Cornwall, the Queen ordered that the Order of Precedence for Ladies at Court should be as follows:

The Queen
The Princess Royal (Her Majesty's daughter)
Princess Beatrice (Her Majesty's granddaughter)
Princess Eugenie (Her Majesty's granddaughter)
Princess Alexandra (Her Majesty's cousin)
The Duchess of Cornwall (wife of the Heir Apparent)

## The Order of Succession to the Throne

The Prince of Wales
Prince William of Wales
Prince Henry of Wales
The Duke of York
Princess Beatrice
Princess Eugenie
The Earl of Wessex
Viscount Severn
Lady Louise Windsor
The Princess Royal
Peter Phillips
Zara Phillips
Viscount Linley

Lady Sarah Chatto
The Duke of Gloucester
The Duke of Kent
[Excludes Prince Michael of Kent, who renounced his place in
the Line of Succession when he married a Roman Catholic.]

Peter and Zara Phillips, children of the Princess Royal, are the only non-titled commoners in the Line of Succession at numbers 11 and 12. Viscount Linley and Lady Sarah Chatto are the children of the late Princess Margaret and the Earl of Snowdon.

## Pages

The senior domestic posts in the Royal Household are the Pages. There are three sets: Page of the Chambers, Page of the Presence and Pages of the Backstairs. This latter is the most desirable as they work closer to the Queen than anyone else, apart from her dressers.

There are five Pages of the Backstairs (the title originated in the days when certain visitors to the Sovereign were 'smuggled' up the backstairs, instead of being brought in through the usual entrance). Four of the Pages wait personally on Her Majesty (the fifth is Deputy Page of the Chambers) working on alternate days in her private apartments and they act as conduits between the Queen and other members of the Royal Family and the Household.

The Page of the Chambers is number two in the Palace hierarchy of domestic servants, second only to the Palace Steward (see Palace Steward). This Page organises the footmen and attendants, including nurses, medical staff and ambulances needed when an Investiture is taking place.

Included in the third set of Pages are the three Pages of the Presence, who, despite their title, do not work personally for the Queen, but mainly for senior members of the Household, performing such mundane but essential tasks as arranging fresh supplies of stationery on the desks of the private secretaries every morning. The title Page of the Presence refers to their original role of working in the Presence Chamber, where the Sovereign dined in State.

Every Page has started as footman and been promoted through merit; there is no longer any nepotism in staff positions as was once the case in almost every department

## Pages of Honour

When the Queen attends the State Opening of Parliament, four young Pages of Honour, usually the sons of friends or members of the Royal Household support her. They wear a knee-length scarlet coat over a white, lace jabot and waistcoat, white stockings, black, buckled shoes and a small sword.

Between them they carry the long heavy train of Her Majesty's robes. At the Garter Service, only two are required because the mantle the Queen wears is not so cumbersome.

In Scotland, where the Queen attends the Order of the Thistle, a boy from a Scottish family is selected to be her Page of Honour.

The Pages serve for two or three years and they have to be between the ages of 12 and 15, after that they are expected to have grown too tall. They do not receive a salary, but they do get an honorarium.

At the Queen's coronation, one of the Pages of Honour, who carried the coronet of the Lord High Chancellor, was a young Master Andrew Parker Bowles.

## Palace Steward

The Palace Steward is the senior liveried domestic servant of the Queen, who controls dozens of staff from his office on the ground floor of Buckingham Palace. He has worked his way up, having started as a junior footman and spent years gaining experience and confidence.

Together with the Master of the Household, he organises all royal entertainment and he has been seen several times in television documentaries measuring, with a ruler, the distance between each place setting before State Banquets. His attention to detail is legendary and, like the Master of the Household, he has only one standard – perfection – and all his colleagues know it.

## Picnics

The Queen and her family love picnics, particularly when they are in the Highlands above Balmoral. But their idea of *al fresco* dining is a little different from that usually enjoyed by the rest of us.

In the first place, footmen carry all the paraphernalia required for the meal to a favourite spot and lay it out, with sparkling crystal and china, and the food and drink (chilled white wine and beer) is contained in cool boxes. They then arrange the barbecue and light it so that the Duke of Edinburgh, who insists on 'cooking' the sausages and steaks himself, only has to turn the food over.

Once everything is ready, the footmen retire to a safe distance – but always within calling range – so that the family can enjoy what they believe is a quiet, informal outing in the country. When the meal is finished, the footmen clear everything away, pack the bags, wash the dishes and carry the lot back to the castle, which is sometimes over a mile away. It's all in a day's work.

## Poet Laureate

The Poet Laureate is a part-time member of the Royal Household, for which a small stipend (at present, £5,750 a year) is paid from the Civil List. Ben Jonson was the first holder of the post when James I appointed him. There have been many famous Poets Laureate, including John Masefield, Sir John Betjeman, Ted Hughes, Andrew Motion and Cecil Day-Lewis. They do not have to do anything if they don't want to, but most like to write commemorative verses to mark special royal occasions, such as a Jubilee, birth or marriage – as Ted Hughes did in 1986 when the Duke and Duchess of York were married.

When there is a vacancy for the post, the Prime Minister suggests a number of candidates for the Sovereign's approval. Once the choice has been made, the name is announced in the *London Gazette*.

The current Poet Laureate, Carol Ann Duffy, who took over on 1 May 2009, is the first woman to be appointed. She is also the first Scottish Poet Laureate in the post's 300-year history.

## 20th-Century Poets Laureate

Alfred Austin (1896)
Robert Bridges (1913)
John Masefield (1930)
Cecil Day-Lewis (1968)
Sir John Betjeman (1972)
Ted Hughes (1984)
Andrew Motion (1999)
Carol Ann Duffy (2009)

## Police Bodyguards

The Queen is probably the least protected Head of State in the World, and that is the way she likes it. When she goes out in public, she is accompanied only by her senior personal bodyguard, a Chief Superintendent of the Metropolitan Police Force who – although he always appears dressed in a conservative lounge suit, and is armed – is not a detective or an officer from Special Branch. He is, in fact, a member of the uniformed branch of 'The Met' who happens to wear plain clothes when on duty.

Royal protection officers are chosen for their dedication and discretion and one, James Beaton, who worked for both the Queen and Princess Anne, was awarded the George Cross for bravery when he prevented an attempted kidnapping of the Queen's only daughter in The Mall on 20 March 1974, during which he was shot five times. Beaton remains the only protection officer so far to have fired his gun in anger.

Of course, there are other police officers involved when the Queen and other members of the family are out and about. There is always a back-up vehicle, carrying emergency medical supplies and the ever-present 'blood box' with the correct type of blood for the royal passenger. Police motorcycle outriders both precede and follow the royal car, clearing traffic along the route.

Nevertheless, the Royal and Diplomatic Protection Unit – to give them their full and correct title, as they also protect all the foreign emissaries in London – is a compact and highly efficient group that carries out its duties with the minimum of fuss. When one realises that the White House security detail alone is larger than the entire Royal Household staff, Buckingham Palace would appear to have refined to a supremely sophisticated degree its own protection arrangements.

## Post Office

There has been a Post Office inside Buckingham Palace since 1902, but it was not the first Royal Post office to be opened. A sub-post office had been opened at Sandringham House in 1877, when the Sergeant Footman performed the duties of the postmaster. Twenty years later, an official called the Court Telegraphist was appointed by Queen Victoria to open a sub-post office at Osborne House on the Isle of Wight. However, it wasn't until 1904, during the reign of King Edward VII, that it was thought necessary to open sub-post offices at Windsor and Balmoral, while at the Palace of Holyroodhouse, the sub-post office was opened only for the few weeks the Court was in residence.

It was in 1906 that the Court Telegraphist was promoted to become Court Postmaster and the rank still exists today with the Court Postmaster being based at Buckingham Palace where the Post Office handles over 1,000 items a week, with a dramatic increase at times of celebration such as royal weddings, birthdays or anniversaries, or at times of bereavement.

Every letter, package and parcel that arrives at the Palace is fed through a fluoroscope to check that nothing dangerous or unsuitable is contained within it.

The image of the Queen, which appears on all United Kingdom postage stamps, was designed by Arnold Machin and first appeared on 5 June 1967.

Since then, more than 200 billion stamps bearing the image have been sold, making the Queen's face the most reproduced image in the world.

The Post Office at Buckingham Palace is situated in the basement, or lower ground floor, and is manned all year round, as is the one at Windsor. However, the Post Office at Balmoral opens only when the Court is in residence, usually August, September and part of October, while the sub-post office at Sandringham, opened in 1877, closed permanently in 1968. The sub-post office at the Palace of Holyroodhouse in Edinburgh also opens only when the Queen is there.

Letters from the Royal Family and the Royal Household do not bear stamps but the envelopes are franked with the date of posting and post code in the upper right-hand corner and the Queen's 'EIIR' cypher in the lower left-hand corner. All correspondence posted during a time of Court mourning have envelopes trimmed with black around the edges.

The office of Court Post existed from 1565 until 1793, with the last holder of the post dying in office in 1812 when the post was abolished. It was King Edward VII who revived royal franking in 1901 and, a year later, he gave permission for the post office to be opened at Buckingham Palace.

Letters written by the Queen do not pass through the post office in the usual way; there is a routine that has been refined over the years so that recipients can be sure the letters are received in pristine condition and not subject to any form of examination.

Having the writer's initials in the lower left-hand corner of the envelope easily identifies letters written to the Queen by friends and family, and the private secretaries know every one of Her Majesty's closest friends and family, so anyone trying to bypass the system has little chance of success.

## Prime Ministers

Twelve Prime Ministers have served the Queen since she came to the Throne in 1952 (13 if you count the two separate ministries of Harold Wilson).

The first, Winston Churchill, (1951–55) was 65 when he welcomed the 25-year-old Queen for the first time, and his attitude, although perfectly correct, was thought in some quarters to be slightly patronising. The Queen found Churchill irritating at first but, within weeks, he had fallen under her spell and their relationship warmed thereafter.

Churchill was succeeded by the debonair Sir Anthony Eden, (1955–57) who made very little impression on Her Majesty and his ill-health, exacerbated by the Suez Canal fiasco in 1956, forced an early retirement.

Harold Macmillan (1957–63) was the third Conservative Prime Minister to serve Her Majesty and is best remembered for his 'You have never had it so good' speech.

When Macmillan resigned, he was replaced by Alex Douglas Home (1963–64), the former Earl of Home, who had renounced his title in order to enter the House of Commons.

It was following the election of 1964 that the Queen met her first Labour Prime Minister, Harold Wilson (1964–70), during the first of his two sessions as PM. They were said to have got along famously in spite of public opinion that the Queen, because of her background, would be a natural Conservative.

In fact, it was Edward Heath (1970–74), the next Conservative Prime Minister, who was the most uncomfortable PM the Queen encountered before or since. He was uneasy in her presence and she found him cold and difficult.

Harold Wilson (1974–76) returned as Prime Minister for a second time and resumed his cordial relationship with Her Majesty. During the annual weekend visit to Balmoral that all Prime Ministers make in the summer, Wilson and his wife fitted in perfectly, with Mary Wilson even joining the Queen in washing dishes when they enjoyed a picnic in the grounds.

Alec Douglas Home and Harold Macmillan had previously also been welcome guests, and as they had been steeped in the traditions of the countryside from birth, found the outdoor pursuits of stalking, shooting and fishing as natural as breathing.

When James Callaghan (1977–79) became Prime Minister, he and the Queen occasionally used their Tuesday evening meetings at Buckingham Palace to walk in the gardens when there was no urgent Parliamentary business to discuss.

Margaret Thatcher (1979–90) was, of course, the first and, so far, only female Prime Minister and reports that she and the Queen never got on have circulated for years. Indeed, in July 1986, a newspaper published a story claiming that Her Majesty was unhappy with the way Margaret Thatcher was running the country. The source was said to be the then Buckingham Place Press Secretary, who denied the accusation and his boss, the Queen's Private Secretary, defended him. It was the only time that the Sovereign's alleged political views had been made known, as she is obliged to treat as confidential all her communications with her Prime Minister.

Although the Palace closed ranks and defended the Press Secretary, he left within the year, and there has never been any further evidence that the Queen and Mrs (later Baroness) Thatcher were not compatible. Indeed, it was reported that the Queen occasionally offered Mrs Thatcher a drink during their Tuesday evening meetings, the only Prime Minister to have been given such hospitality.

Margaret Thatcher's successor was John Major (1990–97), during whose period in office the new Sunday opening hours were introduced.

Then came Tony Blair (1997–2007), who wasn't even born when Elizabeth II came to the Throne. Mr Blair is also the only Prime Minister to have cancelled several of the Tuesday evening audiences with the Queen, because of 'urgent Parliamentary business' in the early days of his premiership. It was during his time that the death of Diana, Princes of Wales, occurred and it is believed that it was due in part to his involvement and advice that the Queen and the Royal Family eventually emerged from the furore relatively unscathed.

Gordon Brown (2007–10) was the fourth Labour leader to hold the position under Her Majesty and his tenure was fraught with difficulties. In particular, his Tuesday audiences must have been uncomfortable when discussing such issues as the question of MPs expenses.

Having lost the election in May 2010, Mr Brown resigned, and David Cameron (Conservative) became Prime Minister, although his party did not have an overall majority.

### The Prime Minister's Audience of the Queen

The Tuesday evening audience is regarded as sacrosanct and every Prime Minister jealously guards the privacy of the meeting, which takes place in the Audience Room on the first floor of the Palace. No other person is present. No notes are taken.

Both the Queen's Private Secretary and his opposite number at No.10 wait downstairs and both the Queen and her Prime Minister know this is not a social occasion; no drinks or other refreshment are offered. It is purely for the Queen to be brought up to date on legislative matters and any international issues involving Britain.

But several Prime Ministers have revealed that when they have asked for advice on certain subjects, Her Majesty has been able to guide them saying she has encountered similar problems 'two or three Prime Ministers before you'. After all, she is the most experienced stateswoman in the world.

## Princess Royal

When the Queen conferred the title Princess Royal on her only daughter, Anne, in 1987, she was reviving a style that had not been used for over 20 years. The last Princess Royal had been Princess Mary, the only daughter of King George V, and when she died in 1965, the title was not inherited.

It was Charles I who introduced the style Princess Royal for his eldest daughter, Princess Mary, and it has become custom for the title to be conferred on the Sovereign's eldest daughter. King George VI did not make his daughter, Princess Elizabeth, Princess Royal because, as stated above, there was already a royal lady bearing the title, until her death in 1965, by which time, of course, Princess Elizabeth had become Queen Elizabeth II.

Princess Royal is purely a courtesy title, having no bearing on the holder's rank or place in the order of precedence. However, it is believed that the Queen made Anne the Princess Royal in order to elevate her to a special place within the Royal Family, as at that time, she was lower in the order of precedence of either of her sisters-in-laws, the Princess of Wales and the Duchess of York. The decision was welcomed by many as a sign of recognition of the hard work the Princess had carried out for many years – and also, she was the only one of the three royal ladies who was 'born to the Purple'.

The title Princess Royal is not automatic for the eldest daughter of the Sovereign and neither can it be handed down. So the present Princess Royal will not be able to pass it on to her own daughter, Zara.

## Privy Council

The Privy Council is the oldest part of the Sovereign's Government dating back to Norman times. There are approximately 400 Privy Councillors, because members are appointed for life and do not have to relinquish their roles when they retire from public office. However, the number that meets regularly in the 1844 Room at Buckingham Palace is usually restricted to four or five and the purpose is to obtain the Queen's consent to proposed legislation.

The only times when all Privy Councillors are required to attend are on the accession of a new Sovereign, when they meet in St James's Palace, not Buckingham Palace, and if an unmarried Sovereign declares his or her intention to marry. The last time this happened was in 1839 when Queen Victoria announced her betrothal to Prince Albert.

An unusual, but welcome, aspect of the monthly meetings is that they are always conducted with everyone present standing, even the Queen. This custom dates from 1861 when, as a mark of respect to Prince Albert who had recently died, all members stood, and the tradition has remained. The reason the members, including the Queen, welcome the custom is that it ensures that the meetings do not last too long; everyone is anxious to get the business over and done with as soon as possible.

The Queen appoints the Privy Councillors, who include all Cabinet Ministers and the Leader of the Opposition. High dignitaries of the Church of England such as the Archbishops of Canterbury and York and the Bishop of London are Councillors, as are judges when they become Lords Justice of Appeal.

If Her Majesty is unable to attend the meetings of the Council, two Royal Counsellers of State take her place from among the Prince of Wales, Prince William, Prince Harry and the Duke of York.

## Queen's Piper

Every morning at 9.00am, the Queen's Piper, dressed in full Highland uniform, marches up and down for 15 minutes on the terrace beneath Her Majesty's window, playing Scottish military tunes on the bagpipes. At each of the Queen's homes, Buckingham Palace, Windsor Castle, Balmoral or the Palace of Holyroodhouse, the routine never changes. He accompanies Her Majesty at all times, except to Sandringham.

In Scotland and at Windsor, he also plays at the Queen's dinner table and, in addition, he has responsibility for the 12 pipers who march around the table at State Banquets.

The piper has three tartans: the Ancient Hunting Stewart in the morning, the Royal Stewart in the evening and, while on duty at Balmoral, he wears the Balmoral Tartan at all times. When he is not piping for the Queen, he acts as a Page of the Presence and carries out other duties throughout the day.

As with so many of today's royal traditions, that of having a Queen's Piper began with Queen Victoria, whose first holder of the post was Angus Mackay (1843–54).

## Queen Victoria

Queen Victoria was born Princess Victoria Alexandra of Kent on 24 May 1819 at Kensington Palace. Her parents were Prince Edward, Duke of Kent, and Princess Victoria Mary Louisa of Saxe-Coburg-Saafield, Duchess of Kent.

Private tutors conducted her education with subjects including Latin, French, German, Italian, Geography, Arithmetic and Music.

On 20 June 1837 she became Queen, as her uncle, William IV, had died without leaving any children. Her coronation took place on 28 June 1838 and the new Queen became the first British Monarch to make Buckingham Palace her permanent London home.

Her Majesty married Prince Albert on 10 February 1840 at the Chapel Royal, St James's Palace, and nine children were born: Victoria, the Princess Royal, in 1840 (who became German Empress on her marriage, prompting her mother to become Empress of India on 1 January 1877, as it was unthinkable for the child to have a title superior to that of her mother); Albert Edward, Prince of Wales (later Edward VII, 1841); Alice (1843); Alfred (1844); Helena (1846); Louise (1848); Arthur (1850); Leopold (1853); and Beatrice (1857).

Queen Victoria bought Osborne House on the Isle of Wight in 1844 and added to the family property holdings when she also bought Balmoral in 1852.

Between 1840 and 1882, seven attempts were made on her life, and after Prince Albert died at Windsor on 14 December 1861, the Queen mourned him for the rest of her life.

Her Diamond Jubilee was celebrated in 1897, and she died peacefully at Osborne on 22 January 1901. Her funeral was held at St George's Chapel, Windsor on 2 February 1901 and she was laid to rest beside her husband in the Frogmore Royal Mausoleum.

## Queen Victoria Memorial

Known irreverently as 'The Wedding Cake', the Queen Victoria Memorial that stands immediately in front of Buckingham Palace was designed by the sculptor Thomas Brock and completed in 1911, ten years after the Queen's death. Constructed from 2,300 tonnes of marble, it epitomises all that was glorious about the British Empire during Victoria's reign, with her, of course, supreme Empress over it all.

# ℜ

## Racing

The Royal Family has long enjoyed the sport of kings – and queens. Even Queen Victoria was an enthusiast in her early days, visiting Royal Ascot with Prince Albert and, on one occasion, even breaking a window in the Royal Box when she rushed to see the finish of a race. King Edward VII loved the social aspect of the sport, once describing the Goodwood meeting as 'a little bit of racing with a garden party tacked on'.

The late Queen Mother's horses raced exclusively 'over the sticks' with the Queen preferring 'the flat', so they were never in competition.

Her Majesty's interest began when she was still Princess Elizabeth. She had been given, as a wedding present from the Aga Khan, a racehorse named Astrakhan, which, in 1949 gave her the first of her many winners when the filly won at Hurst Park.

Since then, Her Majesty has been among the sport's most successful owners and breeders, wining her first Classic in 1957 when Lester Piggott rode Carozza to victory in The Oaks.

The Queen has 20–30 horses in training at any one time and, as the cost of each one is around £20,000 a year, it is not too difficult to work out the overall bill.

Horse racing is not a sport for the feeble-hearted, or those with slim wallets. Someone once claimed it was like fitting a tap to your pocket. It is a bottomless pit.

The Queen's racing interests are looked after by John Warren, the son-in-law of the late Earl of Caernarvon, who was Her Majesty's racing manager for over 30 years, until his sudden death in 2001.

'Porchy' Caernarvon (known as Porchy because, until he succeeded to the Earldom, he was Lord Porchester) was said to be the only man who could get straight through to the Queen at any time. Her instructions were that if he rang, he was never to be asked to ring back. And as Her Majesty insists on naming all her horses herself, her racing team have to discreetly guide her when one of her suggestions might contain a double entendre.

The Queen's mares, foals and resident stallions are stabled on the Sandringham Estate where her adviser is Sir Michael Oswald, who took over the responsibility following the death of the Queen Mother, whose racing manager he had been for many years.

As the Queen has been a passionate racing enthusiast nearly all her adult life, she has become an expert able to match her knowledge with anyone in the racing world. She knows what to look for in a horse – its correct shape, bone structure and pedigree. And those closest to her say she is arguably the best judge of a photo finish they have ever seen. At Ascot, the Royal Box is right on the finishing line and when there is a photo finish, she invariably gets it right before anyone else.

Required reading in Her Majesty's breakfast room is the *Racing Post*, the 'Bible' of the racing fraternity. A copy is placed before her every morning – and if she is abroad, the contents are transmitted to her electronically. It is said that if the Queen didn't get her copy of the *Racing Post* first thing, she would suffer 'withdrawal symptoms'.

Unlike most owners, the Queen does not bet on any of her horses, but she does take part in the Royal Box lottery, where the guests all buy a ticket, with the winnings rarely being above £20.

Although Her Majesty has won most of the Classics, including several in France and the United States, where she visits privately to buy horses at the stud of her old friend Mr William Farish in Kentucky, the main prize, the Derby, has so far eluded her. It is her greatest disappointment.

Some of racing's greatest jockeys have worn the Queen's colours (purple body with gold braid, scarlet sleeves and black velvet cap with gold braid), including Sir Gordon Richards (who was knighted in coronation year), Lester Piggott, Willie Carson, Joe Mercer and Doug Smith.

The Queen Mother's favourite jockey was the late Dick Francis, the man who caused her the greatest disappointment when, yards from the finish in the 1956 Grand National, his horse, Devon Loch, suddenly splayed his forelegs and lost the race.

The Queen inherited her racing colours from her father, King George VI, who, in turn, had kept the same colours as his father and grandfather. It was King Edward VII, as Prince of Wales, who registered his colours in 1875, and his successors have carried them ever since.

Prince Charles has his own racing colours: scarlet, with blue sleeves and black cap. These were the colours first used by the last Prince of Wales (later King Edward VIII) in the 1920s. The Princess Royal uses the same colours as the Queen. The Queen Mother's colours were blue with buff stripes, blue sleeves and black cap with gold tassel.

The Queen herself has never ridden in a horse race, but her daughter, the Princess Royal, has done so a number of times, and so, too, has her granddaughter, Zara Phillips.

The question of who pays for the Queen's racing activities has long been a subject for controversial argument. The truth is that every penny comes from her own pocket. It is all private money and nothing is paid for by the public or comes from the Civil List. The racing is run on a business footing, and the Queen pays corporate taxes, just like everyone else in the sport, so everything is controlled on a strict budget.

# Regalia

### St Edward's Crown
Each Sovereign is crowned by the Archbishop of Canterbury with the St Edward's Crown. The Crown is not worn thereafter.

The Crown dates from the coronation of King Charles II. It is made of gold weighing 4lb 15oz, and is set with semi-precious stones which were designed for the coronation of King George V in 1910.

When Elizabeth II was preparing for her coronation in 1953, she spent hours walking around with a weight similar to the crown on her head so she could become used to it on the day. Someone working in the Palace kitchens said it was like wearing two bags of sugar.

### Imperial State Crown
The Crown was made for Queen Victoria in 1837. It was subsequently remodelled for King George VI's coronation in 1937. The Crown has placed within it perhaps the most precious stones to be found anywhere in the world — the Black Prince's Ruby, the Second Star of Africa and the Stuart Sapphire.

It is worn by the Sovereign on leaving Westminster Abbey after the coronation and at the State Opening of Parliament. The Queen has sometimes referred to it as 'My going-away hat'.

### Great Sword of State
This symbolises the Sovereign's personal sword. It is a two-handed sword of 17th-century design. It is carried at the coronation and at the State Opening of Parliament by a senior peer. On the latter occasion, it is conveyed to Parliament as part of the regalia procession, by the Gentleman Usher to the Sword of State.

### Cap of Maintenance
The Cap of Maintenance is emblematic of high rank and status and forms part of the Crown Jewels. Its exact origin is uncertain but is thought to have originated in the 15th century. It is never worn and is simply carried before the Sovereign at the coronation and State Opening of Parliament.

## The Orb

The Orb – used for every coronation since that of Charles II in 1661 – represents the Sovereign's power and is placed in her right hand by the Archbishop of Canterbury before being returned to the altar.

## The Sceptres

Two Sceptres are used during a coronation, both dating from 1661. The first, the Sovereign's Sceptre with Cross, contains the massive First Star of Africa diamond of 530 carats, and is carried by the Queen in her right hand during the ceremony. The second is the Sceptre with Dove, signifying peace and this is carried in Her Majesty's left hand.

## The Scottish Crown Jewels

The Scottish Crown Jewels consist of a crown, sword and sceptre. The crown was made for James V, and is made of Scottish gold, 22 gemstones and 20 precious stones.

The Sword of State was given to James IV by Pope Julius II in 1507. Four-and-a-half feet long, the blade is etched with the figures of St Peter and St Paul and, until 1987, the sword was used by the Sovereign as part of the ceremony of the Order of the Thistle.

The Sceptre was also a gift from a pope, this time from Pope Alexander VI to James IV in 1494.

In 1953, the Scottish Crown Jewels were formally presented to the Queen and are now on display in Edinburgh Castle.

## The Welsh Regalia

These are the Crown Jewels associated with the Prince of Wales and used mainly for his Investiture. They consist of a coronet, a ring, a rod, a sword and a mantle. The regalia used for the Investiture of Prince Edward (later Edward VIII) in 1911, was also used for that of Prince Charles in 1969.

# Religion

Elizabeth II is Supreme Governor of the Church of England and Defender of the Faith, the faith being the Protestant religion, a role enjoyed by British Monarchs since Henry VIII broke with the Roman Catholic Church so that he could divorce Catherine of Aragon.

One of the Queen's prerogatives is to appoint archbishops and bishops, but only on the 'advice' of the Prime Minister, who, in turn, seeks guidance from the Archbishops of Canterbury and York.

It was at the first State Opening of Parliament attended by the Queen, in 1952, that she made her public declaration of faith in this form:

> 'I, Elizabeth the Second, do solemnly and sincerely in the presence of God, profess, testify and declare that I am a faithful Protestant, and that I will, according to the true intent of the enactments which secure the Protestant succession to the Throne of my realm, uphold and maintain the said enactments to the best of my powers according to the law.'

For the Queen, this was as solemn a promise as the oath she took at her coronation in 1953, and one she has lived by throughout her reign. Her Majesty is no 'fair-weather' churchgoer. She attends every Sunday wherever she is. When she had use of the Royal Yacht, *Britannia*, a service was held every Sunday morning and at Windsor she receives Holy Communion from her private chaplain, before going to the morning service. No one has yet seen her receive the sacrament in public.

At Balmoral, the Queen attends the nearby church of Crathie; while at Sandringham, during the Christmas break, she worships at the church of St Mary Magdalene in Sandringham Park.

Both the Queen and Prince Philip dislike long sermons and clergymen invited to preach are warned beforehand. Prince Philip is reported to claim that the reason is the 'the soul cannot absorb what the posterior cannot tolerate'.

## Remembrance Sunday

This is the Sunday closest to 11 November each year when the nation, led by the Queen, pays homage to the dead of two World Wars and many other conflicts involving British and Commonwealth servicemen and women.

The focal point is the Cenotaph in Whitehall and, just before 11.00am, Her Majesty and other members of the Royal Family – the Duke of Edinburgh in the uniform of an Admiral of the Fleet, the Prince of Wales, the Duke of York, the Earl of Wessex, the Princess Royal and the Duke of Kent, all in service uniform – emerge to take up their positions in front of the Cenotaph.

At the first stroke of eleven o'clock from Big Ben in the Palace of Westminster, a gun of the King's Troop Royal Horse Artillery, located on nearby Horseguards, fires a single round to mark the start of the traditional two-minute silence.

A second round breaks the silence and Her Majesty then places her wreath at the foot of the Cenotaph, followed by the other members of the Royal Family. The Prime Minister and Leader of the Opposition and other politicians then place their wreaths, followed by the representatives of the Commonwealth countries and the other organisations, such as the police, Transport for London and service chiefs and the Royal British Legion.

The Bishop of London then conducts a short service and, when the royal party has retired at 11.30am, a march-past by thousands of ex-servicemen and women begins, to the accompaniment of the regimental bands on duty playing familiar tunes. It is a most touching and moving occasion and one that is watched on television by an audience of millions.


## Royal Ascot

There has been a royal racecourse at Ascot since 1711 when it was built on the orders of Queen Anne. Subsequent Monarchs have blown hot and cold about horse racing, with King Edward VII setting the pattern for Royal Ascot Week that is nowadays celebrated each April.

For the first four days of the meeting – Tuesday, Wednesday, Thursday and Friday (Saturday is a normal race day not attended by Royalty) – the Queen and her guests, who have been staying at Windsor Castle, leave at 1.35pm on the dot and are driven in cars to the Ascot Gate of Windsor Great Park. There they transfer to open, horse-drawn carriages for the procession down the course to the Royal Box. As they are driven past the grandstand, the military band on duty plays the National Anthem.

Her Majesty and her guests occupy the finest viewing position and there is a small dining room immediately behind the Royal Box, where footmen serve afternoon tea. There is also a small television set so that the Duke of Edinburgh, who is not a great fan of racing, can watch cricket if there is a match being played.

The rules applied to people attending Royal Ascot and, by special invitation, allowed in the Royal Enclosure, have been relaxed over the years. Divorced men and women were barred until 1955; if that same rule applied today, the crowd would be very sparse indeed. But undischarged bankrupts and those who have served a prison sentence are not permitted to apply for an entrance voucher, which must be obtained from: Her Majesty's Representative, Ascot Office, St James's Palace, London SW1A 1BQ. In theory, anyone else may apply.

Ladies are required to wear day dress, with hats being obligatory; smart trouser-suits have been tolerated, but not encouraged, since 1970, but jeans or shorts are not acceptable. Gentlemen should wear morning dress, uniform or national dress.

The freehold of the racecourse is owned by the Commissioners of Crown Lands and leased back by the Queen and administered on her behalf by her Representative and the Trustees of the Ascot Authority. No alterations to the course or the buildings is allowed without first obtaining Her Majesty's consent.

## Royal Box at Covent Garden

The most exclusive seats at any theatre in London are those in the Royal Box. At the Royal Opera House in Covent Garden, the Royal Box is reserved for the family alone, with a strict pecking order for those who are entitled to make use of it. The Queen, of course, is number one, but she never goes privately to the opera, so the Prince of Wales, who is a devotee, has first choice and every other member of the Royal Family has to defer to him.

When he attends a performance, there is as much preparation behind the scenes as there is on stage. He always takes a party of guests with him and, hours before, footmen from Clarence House will arrive to set up supper in the private dining room that adjoins the Royal Box. All the food and wine are brought from his own kitchens with crystal glassware, priceless china and silverware laid out on pristine white, linen tablecloths.

During the first interval, the royal party eat the first two courses, and then pudding and coffee is served during the second. Occasionally, other patrons wonder why the curtain has taken a little longer than usual to go up after the intervals; it is because Prince Charles and his guests haven't quite finished their supper.

If another member of the Royal Family has reserved the box on the same night that Prince Charles wants to go, they have to give away. If there is room, he may ask them to join his party, but if not, they are told their evening's entertainment is off. Even if he decides to go at the last minute, his plans invariably come first.

## Royal Household

The Queen employs around 330 full-time staff at her residences and a further 250 honorary and part-timers. The majority of the full-time staff is domestic, with many of the part-timers being temporary attendants brought in when Buckingham Palace is open to the public in August and September.

Among those working full-time, there are distinct divisions. Right at the top are the Members – heads of departments such as the Private Secretary, Keeper of the Privy Purse, Master of the Household and Crown Equerry.

Next in line are the Officials – the administrators, office managers, accountants, clerks and assistant press officers.

Finally, there are those who come under the heading Staff. These include footmen, housemaids, cleaners, cooks, chauffeurs, gardeners and all manual workers.

They all work under the overall supervision of the Head of the Royal Household, the Lord Chamberlain.

Eight Lord Chamberlains have so far served the Queen during her reign.

| | |
|---|---|
| The Earl of Clarendon | 1952 |
| The Earl of Scarbrough | 1952–1963 |
| Lord Cobbold | 1963–1971 |
| Lord Maclean | 1971–1984 |
| The Earl of Airlie | 1984–1997 |
| Lord Camoys | 1998–2000 |
| Lord Luce | 2000–2006 |
| Lord Peel | 2006– |

Even though the Lord Chamberlain is Head of the Household, he does not have a department of his own to run on a day-to-day basis. The office that bears his name is organised by the Comptroller of the Lord Chamberlain's Office, with his boss simply presiding over the monthly department meetings. In the past, the post has been mainly part-time, with the Lord Chamberlain acting as the channel of communication between the House of Lords and the Sovereign and also being Chancellor of the Royal Victorian Order.

One of the perks of being Lord Chamberlain is that he is allocated a splendid apartment in St James's Palace. One of the disadvantages is that he, together with the Lord Steward (see Lord Steward), has to learn how to walk backwards when preceding the Queen and her guest of honour into the State Ballroom at a State Banquet. They are not allowed to turn their backs on the Sovereign, and Lord Chamberlains quickly learn the secret is to follow the pattern on the carpet, at the same time maintaining eye contact with the Queen.

A white staff is the Lord Chamberlain's symbol of office, which he breaks over the grave of a deceased Sovereign. He also carries a key in his hip pocket, but nobody quite knows which lock the key is supposed to open.

Only one holder of the post has not been a peer when he was appointed, Sir Charles Maclean (1971–84). The Queen quickly resolved the problem by making him Lord Maclean immediately. As the Fount of all Honours, she was perfectly entitled to do this. Lord Camoys (1998–2000) was the first Roman Catholic to be appointed Lord Chamberlain in the reign of Elizabeth II.

Even though the Lord Chamberlain is the titular head of the household, no one is left in any doubt that the most important post is that of Private Secretary to the Queen. He is the man who controls her programme, makes all arrangements for her overseas tours and liaises with his opposite number in the Prime Minister's office.

To date, eight Private Secretaries have served her Majesty.

| Sir Alan Lascelles | 1952–53 |
| Sir Michael Adeane | 1953–72 |
| Sir Martin Charteris | 1972–77 |
| Sir Philip Moore | 1977–86 |
| Sir William Heseltine | 1986–90 |
| Sir Robert Fellowes | 1990–99 |
| Sir Robin Janvrin | 1999–2007 |
| Christopher Geidt | 2007– |

## Royal Library

Guests of the Queen at Windsor Castle are often taken to the Royal Library, a treasure house of books, papers and artefacts dating back many centuries. Her Majesty, with the help of the Royal

Librarian, selects items that she thinks will be of special interest to her guests. A military man might see some rare examples of old medals and war maps; an artist would undoubtedly be conducted around the magnificent collection of Old Master drawings.

The possibilities are vast and fascinating. Where else would you find the undershirt worn by Charles I at his execution in 1649, the original of the last letter he wrote, or his Christening robe? Or a clock given as a present to Anne Boleyn by Henry VIII, and Napoleon's letter of surrender written in 1815, or, more recently, the flying gloves worn by Prince Andrew, Duke of York, during the Falklands Campaign of 1982?

The Royal Library is housed in a first-floor suite of rooms on the north side of the Upper Ward of Windsor Castle, adjoining the State Apartments. There are three main rooms containing thousands of books and printed manuscripts, including the Mains Psalter, only the second book to be printed, in 1457, using moveable metal type, and the first to be printed in red and black.

Among the staff that works under the supervision of the Royal Librarian is the Bibliographer, who is responsible for all the books, coins and medals and for arranging exhibitions both within royal residences and, on occasion, at outside venues.

The Chief Binder looks after the maintenance of the books in the Royal Collection with a small team of Binders. Together, they also handle specialist work such as preparing leather binding for books and albums the Queen decides to give to important guests during a State Visit.

The Chief Paper Restorer, as his title implies, has responsibility for restoring and conserving anything on paper in the Royal Collection. This highly specialised craft includes the careful conservation of Old Master drawings, watercolours and prints, some of which are hundreds of years old and can often be in a delicate condition.

All these specialists work under the Royal Librarian who combines his role with that of being Assistant Keeper of the Royal Archives (the Keeper is the Queen's Private Secretary). The Archives are housed in the Round Tower at the Castle, where the photographic curator also works, and where serious researchers are allowed to see various manuscripts under certain conditions.

Very ancient items must be handled while wearing gloves, no notes can be written on the papers and only pencils are permitted to be used for research notes.

The Royal Library is not open to the public, but authors and historians with impeccable credentials are welcomed to this unique collection.

## Royal Lodge

Situated in Windsor Great Park, Royal Lodge is an elegant country house that has replaced the original 18th-century brick property built in the Queen Anne style. Different generations of Royalty have lived there and made many alterations, including the Duke of Cumberland and the Prince Regent (in 1811) who, when he became King George IV in 1820, changed the name of the house from King's Lodge to Royal Lodge.

William IV demolished part of Royal Lodge and, for 60 years, senior members of the Royal Household used it mainly as a 'grace-and-favour' home.

In 1931, King George V gave permission for his son, Prince Albert, the Duke of York, and his wife to take over the property and they moved in the following year, using Royal Lodge as a private country house, even after the Duke and Duchess became King George VI and Queen Elizabeth. They loved the place so much that, after His Majesty's death in 1952, his widow continued to live at weekends at Royal Lodge until she died in 2002. Since then, her grandson, the present Duke of York, has occupied the Lodge and his daughters, Princesses Beatrice and Eugenie, love the place as much as he does.

The gardens reflect the character of the late Queen Mother, who spent many hours working there, and also in the grounds are Y Bwthyn Bach (see Y Bwthyn Bach) and the Royal Chapel of all Saints.

## St George's Chapel

St George's is the chapel of the Order of the Garter (see Garter Service) and the building dominates the Lower Ward of Windsor Castle. Visitors, who enter by the King Henry VIII Gate in Thames Street, are confronted by this magnificent edifice, which was completed by Henry VIII in 1528, after being started by Edward IV in 1475.

St George's is a Royal Peculiar, with the Dean of Windsor, who lives in a house attached to the chapel, answerable only to the Sovereign, rather than to a bishop. The Dean, canons, priests and their staff form the College of St George who hold services every day that are open to the public, except when the chapel is required for a royal occasion.

The Chapel Choir consists of boys from St George's School and Lay Clerks, who live in houses in the Horseshoe Cloister near the great West Door of the Chapel.

St George's has been a burial place for Royalty for centuries, both inside the body of the Chapel itself and in the King George VI Memorial Chapel adjoining the north choir aisle.

Among the more recent royal weddings held in the chapel, two were particularly high-profile – that of the Earl and Countess of Wessex, and the service of blessing that followed the civil ceremony of the Prince of Wales and the Duchess of Cornwall at Windsor Town Hall.

## St Giles Cathedral

As the Church of Scotland does not appoint bishops, St Giles, in the Royal Mile in Edinburgh, is not, strictly speaking, a cathedral. But it is still the most important religious building in Scotland and the Scots are rightly proud of its prestige and association with Royalty.

It was given its name by the Bishop of St Andrews in 1243 and, in the 16th century, St Giles became prominent in the Reformation with John Knox becoming its first Protestant minister. Both Charles I and Charles II briefly restored the cathedral as a bishopric, before it returned to its place as the 'mother church of Presbyterianism'.

The Cathedral contains the Chapel of the Order of the Thistle, where a service is held every year attended by the Queen and the Duke of Edinburgh. They sit in their own stalls in the Royal Pew in the Preston Aisle (built in 1454), with nearby the stalls of the Knights of the Thistle, over which hang their Household banners.

St Giles is one of the most important places of worship in Britain and it becomes the focus of national attention during State ceremonial, and particularly when the Church of Scotland holds its General Assembly in the third week in May.


## Salutes

Gun salutes are fired in Britain to mark certain royal occasions:

| Accession Day | 6 February |
| The Queen's Birthday | 21 April |
| Coronation Day | 2 June |
| The Queen's Official Birthday | A Saturday in June |
| The Duke of Edinburgh's Birthday | 10 June |

The military saluting bases are sited in London, Edinburgh, Cardiff and Belfast.

Salutes are also fired at the State Opening of Parliament when the Queen arrives at the House of Lords and for royal births. When a Head of State pays a State Visit to Britain, a Royal Salute is fired in Green Park.

In London, the King's Troop, Royal Horse Artillery, fire their guns in Hyde Park, with the Honourable Artillery Company parading at the Tower of London.

Royal Navy ships and shore batteries in various locations also fire salutes.

The number of rounds fired on these occasions varies according to the importance. The basic Royal Salute is 21 rounds, with an extra 20 added when the Salute is fired in Hyde Park because it is a 'royal' park. At the Tower of London, they fire 62 rounds on royal anniversaries, the basic 21, plus an extra 20 because the Tower is a Royal Palace and then an additional 21 for the City of London. Indeed, the Tower holds the record for the largest number of rounds fired in a Royal Salute, with a total of 124 fired on those days when the Queen's official birthday falls on 10 June, the same day as the Duke of Edinburgh's birthday.

The first round of a Royal Salute is fired at 12 noon on the dot, except on the occasion of the Queen's official birthday, when it is fired at precisely 11.00am to coincide with Her Majesty's arrival on Horseguards where she takes the salute at the Trooping the Colour Parade. The clock above Horseguards also begins its eleven o'clock chimes at exactly that moment; cynics suggest that the clock is manually prevented from striking too early or late, in order to emphasise the superb timing of the event.

When a Guard of Honour with a military band on parade gives a Royal Salute, the whole first verse of the National Anthem is played if the Queen and the Duke of Edinburgh are present. If only other members of the Royal Family are there, just the first six bars are played. If the Duke of Edinburgh is present with Her Majesty, and he is in uniform, he will acknowledge the salute by returning it on her behalf. If other family members are in uniform, they do not salute.

## Salaries

Nobody joins the Royal Household to get rich. Or if they do, they are soon disappointed as only half-a-dozen of the Queen's servants receive six-figure salaries, nowhere near what they could earn in the private sector of industry and commerce.

Based on official figures released at the end of 2009, the highest paid is the Keeper of the Privy Purse (the man who controls the royal cheque book) who is paid £187,000 a year. He is followed by Her Majesty's Private Secretary on £177,000; the Master of the Household, who runs the domestic side of the Palace, gets £107,000; while the man right at the top, the Lord Chamberlain, who heads the Royal Household, is the poorest paid of the top six, pocketing only £78,000 a year. But this is a dramatic increase on the previous year when his salary was just £36,000. However, the office of Lord Chamberlain is mainly ceremonial and is not regarded as a full-time appointment.

Two of the most important posts in the Household are the Director of Finance and the Director of Property Services. Professionals occupy both these positions and the value the Queen places on them is reflected in their salaries, which are in the grade £90,000–£100,000. Further down the ladder, another six employees are paid between £60,000– £70,000, with a total of 23 earning in excess of £60,000 a year. These are the senior managers such as the Press Secretary to the Queen, the Director of Royal Travel and the Crown Equerry, who each control important departments.

The salaries for the top people are set in accordance with Senior Civil Service pay scales and those who have accommodation provided have rent deducted from their pay. At the time of writing it is 17 per cent.

The men and women who work for the Prince of Wales, across the road from Buckingham Palace at Clarence House, are paid considerably more than those directly employed by the Queen. This is because the money comes from the income of the Duchy of Cornwall, not from the Privy Purse. For example, Prince Charles's Private Secretary is believed to be paid around £300,000 a year, nearly twice that of his counterpart at Buckingham Palace. And the Communications Secretary (equivalent to the Press Secretary) is said to receive nearly three times the salary of his opposite number in the Queen's press office.

Those right at the bottom of the pay ladder – the footmen, housemaids, chauffeurs and cleaners at the Palace – start on the modest basic salary of £11,000 a year rising to £15,000. Senior footmen and Head Housemaids (and there are only three of them) can earn £17,000 a year. They also receive free uniforms and meals while on duty and accommodation for which, as with the senior servants, they pay 17 per cent of their wages in rent. Single men and women are allocated rooms at Buckingham Palace (or one of the other royal residences) while married couples, who may live in 'grace-and-favour' homes outside the Palace, also have to pay Council tax on top of their rent.

The best paid of the domestic staff are those who work in the kitchens. Cooks can earn up to £20,000 after ten years' service, and the Royal Chef is paid around £50,000.

There is one great perk available to everyone who works for the Queen, no matter how humble the position. Once they have left after satisfactory service, a reference written on Buckingham Palace-headed stationery is a virtual guarantee of a well paid job on the outside – usually at far better rates of pay. One footman left after three years' service and secured a post as butler to an American oil billionaire in Texas at $75,000 a year, plus a house and car.

## Standards

The Royal Standard is the Sovereign's personal flag of office and is never flown at half-mast, because the Monarchy never dies. Hence the call, 'The King (or Queen) is dead, long live the King (or Queen).'

The Royal Standard flies wherever Her Majesty is in residence, so you can always tell if she is at home, and also on her car when she is travelling on official duty but not when she is on a private visit. The captain of any aircraft in which Her Majesty is flying is handed a small version of the Standard, which he then attaches to the front exterior of his flight-deck while the aircraft is on the ground. If the Queen is visiting a building, the person responsible for the occasion may also fly the Royal Standard, if he has obtained permission from Her Majesty's Private Secretary, but cathedrals, abbeys and churches may not fly the standard unless they are 'Royal Peculiars' (see Westminster Abbey).

The Royal Standard is divided into four quarters, with two for England (three lions passant), one for Scotland (one lion rampant) and one for Ireland (a harp). Wales is not represented on the Royal Standard as its unique position within the United Kingdom as a separate Principality means it is included in the arms of the Prince of Wales.

The Royal Standard that flies above Buckingham Palace measures 12ft by 6ft, except on ceremonial occasions, when a larger version is flown. There is also a smaller standard that can be hoisted during inclement weather.

## State Banquets

The Queen is reported to have remarked at a State Banquet, when one of her relations complained about the quality of the food, 'Nobody comes here because of the food, but to eat off gold plates.' Whether the story is true or apocryphal, it is perfectly true that gold plate is displayed on the walls of the State Ballroom, where all State Banquets are held, and used on the dining tables together with gold cutlery, vases and candelabra.

The table glass is English cut-crystal, made for the coronation in 1953, and each glass is engraved with the Royal cypher 'E11R'. The dress code is white tie and tails, worn with decorations for gentlemen, and full-length ball gowns and tiaras for the ladies.

Following a reception in the Music Room, the guests move into the State Ballroom and wait for the royal procession to enter. These splendid occasions are held on the first evening of a State Visit by an overseas Head of State (there are usually two every year) and the guests are seated at a long table arranged in a horseshoe shape. The Queen sits in the centre of the head of the horseshoe, with the guests of honour and other members of the Royal Family on either side.

There is a system of 'traffic lights' to control the serving of the courses and old hands at these functions know they should eat as quickly as possible as once the Duke of Edinburgh, a notoriously fast eater, has finished, all plates are removed.

During the meal, a band from the Household Division plays selections of light music up in the gallery above the Ballroom, where, on very warm evenings, it is said to resemble the 'Black Hole of Calcutta'.

The entertainment concludes with 12 pipers from the Scots or Irish Guards who process around the dining table playing quick marches and then leave.

Coffee and liqueurs are served to the guests in the State Apartments and the evening is usually over by 11.00pm.

## Swan Upping

All swans in Britain are the property of either the Queen, as Seigneur of the Swans, or two livery companies: the Worshipful Company of Vintners and the Worshipful Company of Dyers.

Once a year, in July, their representatives, together with the Lord Chamberlain, or someone from his office, set out in boats on a stretch of the River Thames between Sunbury and Pangbourne to mark the swans. Whenever a cob and hen with a group of cygnets is sighted, the cry 'Up, Up, Up . . .' rings out and the group is herded gently into the bank of the river for the cygnets to be marked. If there are four, for example, two will be marked for the Queen and one each for the Livery Company.

The Office of Keeper of the Queen's Swans has resided in the Turk family of watermen for generations and the 'Uppers' – the men who actually catch and mark the swans – are very fit and experienced boatmen.

The Swan Keeper wears a uniform of scarlet jacket, white trousers and a peaked cap with a badge of the Royal Crown. On his left arm is another badge with the words 'Her Majesty's Swan Keeper' encircling an image of a swan. The Vintners Swan Marker wears a green jacket, while the Dyers Swan Marker wears a distinctive coat in blue with gold braid.

As their boats pass Windsor Castle, they all stand to attention with oars raised in salute. Newcomers from the Lord Chamberlain's office sometimes find this part of the ceremony a little difficult – to the amusement of the old-timers.

## Swimming Pool

The swimming pool at Buckingham Palace is located at the rear, northern part of the building. All the royal children were taught to swim there but today it is used mainly by the Duke of Edinburgh who still likes to do his 'daily laps'. Members of the Household are permitted to use the pool with the rule being that if one of the staff is already in when a member of the Royal Family arrives, he or she will immediately get out, unless invited to remain, which often happens. If any of the Household arrives to find one of the Royal Family already swimming, they do not enter the pool until it has been vacated.

The Queen is an accomplished swimmer and diver, who, although she no longer uses the pool as frequently as she once did, was taught to swim at an early age in the Palace's pool. The instructor was a formidable lady named Miss Daly, who used to tie a length of rope around the princess's waist and then hold a long wooden pole just in front of her as she splashed along, gradually releasing the rope until the young Elizabeth suddenly found she no longer needed it and she was swimming unaided. Miss Daly's proud boast was that she had never had a single failure.

Princess Elizabeth showed no fear of the water, either in swimming or diving, and she went on to an advanced level, winning a silver medal for life saving when she was still a very young girl.

# T

## Tartans and Tweeds

Whenever members of the Royal Family travel to Scotland they tend to 'go native'. In other words, they don the kilt, wear tartans and tweeds and carry rough sticks when out walking. Indoors, their entertainment is also strictly Scottish with traditional country dances being the order of the day when guests are invited to an evening function.

Balmoral Castle is decorated with tartan wallpaper; curtains, carpets and even some of the bedclothes reflect the Highland theme. On the first occasion the Duke of Edinburgh visited Balmoral, he wore a borrowed kilt and made a short curtsey to his father-in-law, King George VI. His Majesty was not amused. The Duke now wears the tartans of the Queen's Own Highlanders (formerly the Cameron Highlanders which merged with the Seaforth Highlanders in 1961) and the old Cameron Highlander's tartan. The Prince of Wales, who is known in Scotland as the Duke of Rothesay, favours a kilt worn by the Gordon Highlanders, of which he is Colonel-in-Chief. He also wears on occasion a special tartan as Lord of the Isles, another of his titles.

The most recognisable of the 'royal' tartans is the Royal Stewart with its red-based pattern. But there are several variations of the Royal Stewart, including the dress tartan, worn with evening wear, with a white background, and the Hunting Stewart, with a green background, worn during the daytime particularly, as the name implies when the wearer is out stalking or hunting. The Princess Royal is often seen wearing this form of tartan. The Queen wears skirts in tartan, one of which is known as Ancient Tartan.

The grey-and-red Balmoral Tartan is exclusive to the Royal Family. Edward VIII registered the design in 1936 to prevent anyone else using it.

There is nothing very ancient about the Balmoral Tartan, being invented by Queen Victoria and Prince Albert in 1850, the two originators of the 'Scottish' theme, when they bought Balmoral in 1848.

Another exclusive design is that of Balmoral Tweed. King George VI invented this lovat-coloured tweed in 1937 (the year of his coronation) and members of the Royal Family and the Royal Household (with special permission) wear it when shooting at Balmoral and also on the Sandringham Estate. Again no member of the public is allowed to wear the tweed – or even to buy it. The Queen's approval is required each time a bolt of the cloth is issued.

## Tax

Until February 1993, the Queen, as Monarch, was exempt from paying Income Tax on both her Civil List allowance and on her personal assets. However, she informed the then Prime Minister, John Major, that she intended to voluntarily pay Income Tax for the first time. However, she isn't the first Sovereign to pay tax; Queen Victoria, King Edward VII and King George V had all paid some form of Income Tax during their time on the throne, albeit in the days when Income Tax was just a few pence in the pound, rather than the punitive amounts of later years.

We are never going to know how much the Queen pays, as her affairs, in line with every other private individual, are confidential and are never revealed in Palace accounts, but it is generally accepted that she is a higher-rate tax payer. However, The Queen's estate is exempt from paying Inheritance Tax or Capital Transfer Tax on her death, so she will be able to pass on a sizable fortune intact to her heirs.

Her Majesty is liable to pay tax on her private estates at Sandringham and Balmoral – and she does pay tax due to Customs and Excise on gifts she receives while she is on overseas visits. She is also registered for Value Added Tax through the Duchy of Lancaster.

Other members of the Royal Family do not receive any exemptions and are liable to pay tax on their incomes from all sources.

## Telephone Exchange

It is said that the telephonists who man the exchange at Buckingham Palace can find the telephone number of anyone in the world within minutes. They say they have never been stumped and their proud boast is they never will be.

The telephone exchange at Buckingham Palace is on the ground floor at the left of the Palace, as you look at it from the front, next to the guardroom. It operates 24 hours a day, 365 days a year, yet the faces of the four ladies who work there are largely unknown even to other members of the Household. They used to be supervised by a Senior Telephonist, who every morning when the Queen Mother was alive, connected her with the Queen with the immortal words, 'Your Majesty, I have Her Majesty on the line for you.' In recent years, the post of Senior Telephonist has disappeared to be replaced with the more correct, but infinitely less prestigious-sounding, Telephony Manager.

## Television and Radio

These days it is taken for granted that members of the Royal Family appear on radio and television frequently and for a variety of reasons. But it is only since the death of King George VI in 1952 and the coronation of the Queen the following year that royal appearances have become regular and not restricted to special events.

The first member of the Royal Family to broadcast (on radio, which was called 'wireless' in those days) was the then Prince of Wales (later King Edward VIII), when he spoke on station 2LO (which preceded the BBC) on 7 October 1922. The occasion was to address 50,000 boy scouts and his Royal Highness spoke from his study in York House at St James's Palace.

The Prince was a pioneer of royal broadcasting, making the first transmission from the Palace of Westminster on 26 May 1926 and also the first from the Festival of Remembrance service held in the Royal Albert Hall on 26 May 1926. He went on to use the medium of radio many times until, of course, his memorable abdication speech, broadcast from Windsor Castle on 11 December 1936.

His father, King George V, made his first Christmas Day broadcast to the Empire in 1932, having made his broadcasting début on 23 April 1924, when he opened the Empire Exhibition at Wembley.

Other notable dates in royal broadcasting include 12 December 1928, when Queen Mary, whose voice was rarely heard, spoke on the wireless; and 23 May 1924, when the Duke of York (later King George VI) had his introduction to the medium, when his speech to the Royal Colonial Institute at the Hotel Victoria in Northumberland Avenue in London, was broadcast. Of course, in those days, there were fewer than 20,000 wireless sets in Britain.

The Duchess of York (later the Queen Mother) broadcast for the first time when she received the freedom of the City of Glasgow on 21 September 1927 and her acceptance speech was transmitted.

On his accession to the throne in 1936, King George VI was a reluctant broadcaster (or public speaker of any kind) because of his unfortunate, nervous stammer, which plagued him throughout his life. However, he made great efforts to overcome this condition and was forced to make a number of broadcasts, particularly during the Second World War.

It was also during the war that Princess Elizabeth made the first of many broadcasts that were to follow, both on radio and television. She appeared on the BBC's *Children's Hour* programme on 13 October 1940 and, towards the end of the show, she invited her younger sister, Princess Margaret, to join her. She did, uttering just one word: 'Goodnight.'

In those days, almost all broadcasting was 'live' as recording technology was not anywhere near as sophisticated as in later years. And this added to the nervousness of the participants. However, the funeral of King George VI was televised 'live' on 15 February 1952 and, the following year, on 2 June 1953, the coronation of Elizabeth II gave the biggest boost ever to the TV industry when it was shown 'live' in spite of opposition from many quarters, including Winston Churchill and the then Archbishop of Canterbury, who was concerned that 'working men in public houses wearing caps would be able to watch the ceremony'. However, they were all overruled and it was the Queen herself, encouraged by the Duke of Edinburgh, who took the final decision to allow cameras and microphones inside Westminster Abbey and along the processional route.

It was due to that single event that Britain became, almost overnight, a television-obsessed nation. In 1969, the BBC, in spite of early objections by the Queen Mother, broadcast the first major television documentary featuring the Royal Family. Earl Mountbatten was said to be the force behind the idea, aided by Prince Philip and one of the Queen's private secretaries. The programme was an immediate success worldwide and proved to be a triumph of public relations, brilliantly stage-managed from start to finish, and although today it looks stilted and affected, it gave people their first view of the private lives behind the public image.

The Queen has never been totally relaxed in front of the TV cameras. She delivered her first Christmas message, on radio only, on 25 December 1952, but it wasn't until five years later, in 1957, that she spoke 'live' to the Commonwealth on television in what has now become an established annual tradition. Today, the Christmas broadcasts are much more relaxed and informal and show Her Majesty in several different surroundings instead of placing her stiffly in one room. The broadcasts are filmed a few days before transmission, so that any errors or necessary changes can be made before the final version is shown.

Arguably one of the most memorable of all the Queen's television broadcasts was the one she made from Buckingham Palace at the time of the funeral of Diana, Princess of Wales, in August 1997. She spoke movingly of her former daughter-in-law as 'an exceptional and gifted human being'. It was simple and impressive without being over sentimental. It was also one of royal broadcasting's finest moments.

## Thrones

The Throne Room at Buckingham Palace contains the Chairs of Estate used by the Queen and the Duke of Edinburgh during the first part of the coronation ceremony.

For the Crowning itself, Her Majesty sat on St Edward's Chair, which is kept permanently at Westminster Abbey. In fact, it has left the Abbey only once since it was first made in 1300, and that was when it was taken to Westminster Hall in 1653 for the Installation of Oliver Cromwell as Lord Protector.

Another chair used by the Queen during the coronation service was the Chair of Homage to which she moved once she had been crowned, to receive homage from her subjects. This chair is now kept at Windsor Castle in the Garter Throne Room where Her Majesty uses it during the private ceremonies of the Order of the Garter (see Order of the Garter).

On either side of the dais in the Throne Room at Buckingham Palace are the coronation thrones of King George VI and Queen Elizabeth. Elsewhere in the room are the coronation chairs of King George V and Queen Mary, while in the deep window recess is the State Throne of Queen Victoria, who did not possess a Seat of State in the Palace so she ordered one to be made in crimson and gold. The coronation chairs of King Edward VII and Queen Alexandra are located on the dais in the State Ballroom.

When the Queen opens Parliament, she reads her speech from the Throne in the House of Lords that was designed by Pugin in 1834. At the same time, the Duke of Edinburgh sits alongside her in the Chair of State made for Queen Victoria's consort, Prince Albert.

The Throne Room at Buckingham Palace has been used many times for the official wedding photographs of members of the Royal Family, including those of Princess Margaret and Lord Snowdon (1960), Princess Anne and Mark Phillips (1973), the Prince and Princess of Wales (1981) and the Duke and Duchess of York (1986).

As all these marriages ended in divorce, some members of the Royal Household tend to refer to the room (out of the hearing of the Royal Family) as the 'Jinx Room'.

When Prince Edward, Earl of Wessex, married Sophie Rhys Jones, he took no chances and his ceremony and photographs took place at Windsor.

## Titles

Most of the male members of the immediate Royal Family hold subsidiary titles but only one is female and that is the Queen. Her Majesty is also Duke (not Duchess) of Lancaster and Duke of Normandy, in which role the Channel Isles, which retain autonomy in government as a self-governing possession of the English Crown, owe her allegiance.

HRH The Duke of Edinburgh is also Earl of Merioneth and Baron Greenwich, while his eldest son, Charles, easily outstrips him in terms of titles. In addition to his principal title of the Prince of Wales, he is also Earl of Chester, Duke of Cornwall, Duke of Rothesay, Earl of Carrick, Baron of Renfrew, Lord of the Isles and Prince and Great Steward of Scotland.

Prince Andrew, Duke of York, bears the titles of Earl of Inverness and Baron Killyleagh.

The Queen's youngest child, Prince Edward, was created Earl of Wessex and Viscount Severn, the courtesy title now used by his son James, on the day he married Sophie Rhys-Jones. Buckingham

Palace announced at that time that he would become Duke of Edinburgh, the title held by his father since 1947, when the Dukedom reverts to the Crown. Although Edward's children are entitled to be called HRH Prince James and HRH Princess Louise (their legal names) as grandchildren of the Sovereign through the male line of descent, Her Majesty agreed that they should relinquish these styles at the request of their parents who felt it would be more appropriate in the 21st century for them to hold lesser titles.

The son and daughter of Princess Anne, the Princess Royal, and her former husband, Captain Mark Phillips, do not hold any titles at all. Anne decided, against her mother's wishes, not to allow them to be called Prince, Princess or even Lord and Lady.

When Peter Phillips was born in 1977, he was the first grandson of a reigning Sovereign to be born a commoner in more than 500 years.

Zara Phillips has held two titles, both sporting and distinctly non-royal. She was European and World Three-Day Event Champion in the toughest of all equestrian disciplines, when it was said that the horse was the only one present not to know of her royal connections.

## Trains

There is actually no such thing as the 'Royal Train'. At present, there are nine coaches that can be assembled into whatever configuration is required, depending on which member of the Royal Family is travelling, and each time they are described as the Royal Train.

There used to be 14 coaches but, in 1996, this number was reduced with two being retained for spares and three being sold in 2001 for £236,000.

If the Queen and Prince Philip are travelling together then seven carriages are brought into operation, the same number that Prince Charles uses. However, if the Duchess of Cornwall accompanies her husband, then an extra carriage is attached for her staff. This is one of the Duke of Edinburgh's carriages, as the Duchess's bedroom and sitting rooms are located next to those of the Prince of Wales, but separated by a slim partition.

The decoration in the Duchess's bedroom is mainly pink with bird's-eye Maplewood panelling and one request she made when joining the Royal Family was that blackout curtains be fitted to all the windows in her carriages as she does not like any light to filter in during the night. Her adjoining en suite bathroom is also pink in colour.

Prince Charles' bedroom and sitting rooms are masculine in décor with blue being the predominant colour and the pictures, which he chose himself, reflecting his sense of humour and also his love for the former Royal Yacht *Britannia* as a painting of the ship hangs directly over his bed.

The Prince of Wales's Dining saloon is numbered 2916, with the Sleeping Car being 2922.

The Queen's personal saloon, No. 2903, has a bedroom, decorated in light pastel shades and contains a 3ft-wide single bed (there are no double beds on the Royal Train). Her Majesty's adjoining bathroom is equipped with a full-size bath (Prince Philip prefers a shower) while the sitting room, in pale blue, has a sofa, armchairs and a small dining table where the royal couple enjoy breakfast together.

Her Majesty's saloon, where the walls are adorned with paintings of Scottish landscapes and several prints of earlier Royal Train journeys, is easily identified as it is the only one with double doors in the vestibule at its end that open directly on to the platform at any given destination.

The Duke of Edinburgh's saloon, No. 2904, is functional and businesslike as he uses the train very much as a mobile office. One distinction in his bathroom is a magnified shaving mirror at eye level to the right of the lavatory so he can shave while sitting down. There is also a large blown-up version of the Duke's senior rail card, which was given to him when he became eligible on 10 June 1987.

Only four members of the Royal Family are allowed to use the Royal Train in their own right: the Queen, the Duke of Edinburgh, the Prince of Wales and the Duchess of Cornwall. Any other member of the family has to have the permission of Her Majesty before travelling and she is very strict about any possible use that might be seen as frivolous and unnecessary.

The Royal Train is arguably the favourite form of transport for the Royal Family and it has been ever since Queen Victoria became the first reigning Monarch to make a journey by rail in 1842 when she travelled from Windsor to Paddington – with no less a figure than Isambard Kingdom Brunel on the footplate of the locomotive.

The locomotives that power the train are managed by EWS (English Welsh & Scottish Railways), with the saloons operated by Alstom from their base at Wolverton near Milton Keynes, but as both companies were taken over early in 2009 by D.B. Schenker, part of the German State Railway system, the British Royal Train is now entirely German-owned.

The on-board catering remains the responsibility of Rail Gourmet, a subsidiary of the giant Compass catering conglomerate. The only full-time staff are those employed at Wolverton; the stewards who look after the Royal Family work for Virgin Trains when they are not on Royal Train duty, while the engine drivers are drawn from a pool of EWS men. Security is the responsibility of British Transport Police. But, strangely, there is no Royal Train driver as such. Whoever is next on the rota gets the job.

## Travelling Yeoman

An important post within the Master of the Household's Department is that of the Travelling Yeoman. As his title implies, he moves with the Court from Buckingham Palace to Windsor, Sandringham, Balmoral and Holyroodhouse, as well as accompanying Her Majesty on journeys on the Royal Train and on all overseas visits.

His principal task is to help with all travel arrangements, being responsible for all luggage for both the Royal Family and the Household. He also looks after the distribution of newspapers and magazines in all the Royal residences.

## Triplets and Quadruplets

During Queen Victoria's reign, she instituted a custom whereby any mother giving birth to triplets or quadruplets was given a one-off payment. Those with triplets received £3, while those with quads had £4. The idea was to help those parents who were too poor to provide the extra food and clothes needed with the additions to their family.

In 1938, the conditions that the recipients had to be 'poor' were abolished and everyone who had these multiple births received the bounty, as a mark of recognition by the Sovereign.

In 1957, it was decided to discontinue the custom and, instead, these days a message of congratulation from the Queen is sent to the parents.

## Trooping the Colour

The ceremony of Trooping the Colour, held in June every year to mark the Sovereign's official birthday, has its origins in the early 18th century and the form of the parade has changed very little since then.

The parade is held on Horseguards, and is witnessed by several thousand spectators, including invited diplomats, politicians and senior service personnel from Britain and abroad. Tickets are also made available to members of the public who need to apply many months in advance. There are also a number of dress rehearsals carried out in the weeks before the actual parade with exactly the same format and protocol. The only difference being that, on the day, the salute is taken by the Queen; at the rehearsals, a senior army officer performs the duty.

Her Majesty has attended every Trooping the Colour ceremony

since she first came to the throne with the exception of 1955 when, because of a national rail strike, the parade was cancelled.

The Queen, then Princess Elizabeth, first appeared on parade in 1947, the first event following the Second World War, as Colonel of the Grenadier Guards and, in 1951, she deputised for her father, King George VI, who was unable to attend through illness. Between 1969 and 1986, Her Majesty, wearing a scarlet tunic, black skirt and tricorn hat, rode to and from the parade on her horse Burmese. But when he became too old, she decided not to train a replacement and, from that day, she has been driven in a phaeton built in 1842 for Queen Victoria.

It was on 13 June 1981 that a young man leapt from the crowd on the corner of The Mall as Her Majesty was about to enter Horseguards, and fired six shots at her.

They turned out to be blanks but no one, least of all the Queen, realised this at the time, but she retained her composure – as did Burmese – and they continued to the parade as if nothing had happened.

Following the Trooping the Colour parade, the Royal Family gather on the balcony of Buckingham Palace to watch a flypast by aircraft of the Royal Air Force, which often includes the surviving Lancaster, Spitfires and Hurricanes of the Second World War, as well as the latest jets.

# U

## Undertakers

The family firm of Leverton & Co has been taking care of royal funerals for generations. Founded in 1769, there has always been a Leverton at its head and the man currently responsible for co-ordinating the Royal Family's funeral arrangements is Clive Leverton (the eighth generation) from his head office in Camden.

The company has a reputation for discretion and respectful tact and its relationship with Royalty means that they are always ready to cope with any emergency, such as the unexpected death of the late Diana, Princess of Wales, for which there was no precedent.

# Ꝟ

## Valets

Valets (correctly pronounced to rhyme with 'wallet' not 'valay') are the closest personal servants of the male members of the Royal Family, and they are invariably chosen from the ranks of footmen who have distinguished themselves after several years' loyal service. A valet sees his master in the most intimate circumstances and unquestioning discretion is a prime qualification for the job.

Before taking up the post, the Deputy Master of the Household explains in minute detail the requirements of the person they are about to work for. And before being promoted to the personal staff of a member of the Royal Family, a valet will first of all be attached to a senior member of the Royal Household, who can be far more demanding than the Royals on occasion.

New equerries appointed to the Palace sometimes assume a mantle of grandeur, getting ideas far above their station, ordering the valet to wash dirty shirts and underwear, vacuum carpets left muddy after boots have been worn and to clear away drinks and food left over from a party held the night before. None of these tasks falls within the duties of the valet. If this goes on too long, or if the equerry becomes a little too big for his boots, the Sergeant Footman is informed and he very forcibly explains to the equerry – in plain language – that they are all merely servants of the Queen and should behave as such. The equerry soon gets the message.

The details are quite extraordinary once the valet is appointed, by personal choice, to one of the Royals. He is told the routine to be followed when waking his 'gentleman' in the morning. 'Open the door as quietly as possible. If a light is required, try to switch one on that does not shine in the gentleman's eyes. After drawing back the curtains and closing any open windows, collect the previous evening's clothes in this order: jacket, trousers, in their creases, shirt and underclothes. Socks and bow ties should tucked into one of the shoes so they will not be lost on the way to the pressing room.'

The valet is instructed not to speak until he is spoken to and told how he should lay out the day's outfits, and in what order, so they are handed to the wearer, as they are required.

There are more instructions about how to press garments correctly, with the warning that '...no Savile Row tailor sends out suits with creases in the sleeves'. And if a suitcase is to be packed, the order in which the garments should be folded is prescribed, so they come out of the suitcase ready to be worn immediately.

As many senior members of the Royal Household, as well as the male members of the Royal Family, have service connections, the valet is taught how to lay out ceremonial uniforms and he is also sent to Spink, the renowned medal specialists, to learn the correct order in which to attach decorations.

As every royal male enjoys country sports, his valet has to learn how to load a shotgun, so he goes to either Purdey or Holland and Holland, the royal gunsmiths, for a short course of tuition. He is also measured for a suit of clothes to be worn in the field.

Each of the men in the Royal Family has his own little peculiarities. Prince Philip and Prince Charles will only write using a favourite fountain pen, so their valets carefully pack them for overseas visits, making sure there is plenty of blotting paper wrapped around them in case they leak at high altitude.

Prince Charles likes to shave before landing after a long-haul flight, so a battery electric shaver is always in the hand luggage.

Prince Philip's valet makes sure he has a spare pair of reading glasses on him at all times.

And the one essential item that every valet packs on every overseas trip is a complete set of morning clothes, so that if a death in the Royal Family should occur when they are travelling, his master can return to Britain suitably clad.

There is a special bond between the royal men and their valets. Prince Charles has often said he could do without practically anyone in his Household except his valet. He has three. They know secrets such as the kind of music their master likes to listen to in his car, what his favourite food is – and they hear what he feels about other people, particularly some public figures. They choose the clothes he is going to wear that day – the shirts, ties, socks and even cufflinks. One Royal valet was rebuked when he asked his boss which tie he would prefer, only to be told, 'You choose. That's what I pay you for.' He didn't make the same mistake again.

Discretion is taken for granted, as is loyalty. But even though the valet sees his master in the most private circumstances, he must never forget for a moment who is master and who is servant. Democracy goes only so far.

## Vice-Chamberlain of the Household

The holder of this post is appointed by Parliament to the Royal Household and the appointment changes with each Government. As a member of the Chief Whips office, his duties are mainly political, but one of his Household tasks is to write, before dinner, every day, an account of proceedings in the House of Commons up to that time, and despatch it to Buckingham Palace for the Queen to read. It is confidential and only she sees it. Until fairly recently, the report was sent in a dispatch box; now it is transmitted electronically from the Palace of Westminster, and received via e-mail at Buckingham Palace.

One other unusual and ancient custom involving the Vice-Chamberlain is that, at the State Opening of Parliament, he is the only MP who does not remain in Parliament. Instead, he is required to place himself as a 'hostage' at Buckingham Palace, until the Queen returns safely. During the ceremony, he joins the Lord Chamberlain – his theoretical 'keeper' – and they enjoy a cup of coffee or something a little stronger, until the royal procession arrives back in the Forecourt of the Palace.

## Victoria Cross

The highest award for gallantry ranks above all other medals and decorations and can be awarded to British and Commonwealth forces and, in special cases, to civilian personnel serving in the Merchant Navy.

Queen Victoria ordered that the VC should be brought into service and it was instituted on 29 January 1856, originally only to members of the Royal Navy and British Army. Subsequent royal warrants were introduced to allow officers, NCOs and men (and women, though no female has been awarded the VC at the time of writing) to be eligible for the medal for outstanding gallantry in the face of the enemy, regardless of rank. So, in the 19th century, when different grades of medal were awarded to officers and other ranks, the VC became the first of the truly democratic awards for bravery.

Although the award was first gazetted in 1856, its first recipient received it for an act of valour that took place some two years earlier. On 21 June 1854, a 20-year-old Irishman, Charles David Lucas, was serving on board *HMS Hecla*, when he picked up with his bare hands a live Russian shell and threw it overboard, saving the lives of all his shipmates – and the ship itself. Lucas eventually rose to the rank of Rear Admiral, and his name became immortal as the first man to win the coveted Victoria Cross. Since then, nearly 1,500 VCs have been awarded, including those to Gurkha soldiers and members of the Royal Flying Corps in the First World War and later the Royal Air Force.

The medal is made of bronze from Russian guns captured during the Crimean War. Above the royal crown, the obverse bears a lion guardant, and below is the simple inscription: 'For Valour'. On the reverse, the date of the feat for which the medal has been awarded is engraved

The Victoria Cross is worn on a crimson chest ribbon with a mounting with the letter 'V' on the lower side.

Recipients of the award are entitled to a tax-free annuity of £100 for life and to use the letters VC after their name. The VC is also awarded posthumously and can also be forfeited, though only eight have ever been withdrawn and none since 1908.

The equivalent award that can be made in peacetime and wartime, but not during an engagement with the enemy, and to non-service personnel, is the George Cross (see George Cross).

## Visitors' Book

It is possible for anyone to sign the Queen's Visitors' Book at Buckingham Palace to let Her Majesty know they have called in. Until fairly recently, the book was kept in the waiting room on the immediate right as one entered the Palace through the Privy Purse Door (that's the one on the right as you look from the front). It was a unique way of seeing a little of the Palace normally reserved for official visitors.

However, because of security regulations, the book is now kept in the Police Box just inside the North Central Gate but people from all over the world still ask to sign and no one is ever refused. The Queen likes to see some of the signatures and remarks and, from time to time, the book is sent up for her inspection.

# Weddings

## Punctuality

When Prince Charles and Lady Diana Spencer were married in 1981, the then Crown Equerry, Lt Col Sir John Miller, who was responsible for transporting the bride to St Paul's Cathedral, rehearsed the route many times, stopwatch in hand, to make sure everything ran to time. His proud boast was that no member of the Royal Family had ever been late at a destination during his period in office.

He was therefore horrified when, at the last minute, Diana told him she wanted to exercise the bride's prerogative and arrive at the cathedral two minutes late. There was a huge discussion and finally a compromise was reached. He allowed her to turn up just 30 seconds after the allotted time. She was satisfied and he, albeit reluctantly, was happy to oblige the newest member of the family.

## Wedding Breakfasts

As food rationing was still in force in 1947, the wedding breakfast of Princess Elizabeth and Prince Philip reflected the austerity of the day. The meal began with Fillet of Sole Mountbatten – named obviously in honour of the bridegroom – followed by Casserole of Partridge, with the birds all having been shot on the Sandringham Estate, accompanied by green beans, potatoes and salad, again all grown in the royal gardens. The dessert was Bombe Glacée Princesse Elizabeth and coffee. Hardly a ration-book busting feast.

By the time the Queen's only daughter, Princess Anne, was married, for the first time, to Mark Phillips in 1973, restrictions had been lifted and the wedding breakfast was slightly, but only slightly, more sophisticated. They began with scrambled eggs, lobster, shrimps and tomato in mayonnaise, followed by a main course of partridge dressed with fresh mushrooms, peas, cauliflower and new potatoes, with a salad afterwards and a dessert of Bombe Glacée Royale, which was peppermint ice-cream filled with grated chocolate. An ice-cream dish is often a favourite at royal meals.

On 29 July 1981, the wedding of the decade took place when the Prince and Princess of Wales were married. Their celebration breakfast started with quenelles of brill in a lobster sauce, accompanied by a German wine – Brauneberger Juffer Spätlese 1976. The main course consisted of sautéed chicken breasts, stuffed with lamb mousse, covered in brioche crumbs and served with a creamy, mint-flavoured sauce – the whole being garnished with samphire, a Norfolk seaweed delicacy long enjoyed by the Royal Family when they are at Sandringham. In honour of the bride, the dish was called Supreme de Volaille Princesse de Galles. The vegetables were broad beans, sweetcorn and new potatoes, all washed down with Château Latour 1959.

A salad to refresh the palate was served next, followed by fresh strawberries with Cornish clotted cream, all from Prince Charles's own Duchy of Cornwall farms, with a splendid champagne, Krug 1969, for the toasts, and an excellent Taylor 1955 port to finish off.

The wedding cake had been made by the Royal Navy at their Cookery School at Chatham and measured 5ft (1.5m) high in five tiers and weighed two hundredweight (102kg). And the Navy had made a second identical cake just in case the first was damaged in transit.

**Dresses**

When the Queen, as Princess Elizabeth, married Lieutenant Philip Mountbatten in November 1947, her dress had a fan-shaped train 15ft long, in transparent, ivory silk tulle, with a deep border embroidered with a roses-and-wheat motif.

The main eye-catching feature of the dress was a rose of York, which had been hand-embroidered with more than 10,000 pearls and crystals. The skirt was of ivory Duchesse satin, below a fitted bodice and heart-shaped neckline.

As clothes were still rationed in those early post-war days, the

Prime Minister, Clement Atlee, allowed the bride to have an extra 100 clothing coupons so she would not have to stint on the dress (with 23 for the bridesmaids).

As the dress was designed by the court favourite Norman Hartnell, there is no doubt that he was not going to be restrained by any shortage anyway. The wedding dress is stored in a special airtight, sealed container at Buckingham Palace to maintain its pristine condition.

**Presents**
Prince Elizabeth and Prince Philip were given a total of 1,347 gifts when they married. They came from all over the world, with some being more practical than others. The Princess was given 100 pairs of nylon stockings, this being long before tights were introduced, and a new electric food mixer was sent to the kitchens but none of the chefs knew how to make it work.

Winston Churchill offered a set of books, all written by himself, while Philip's Uncle Dickie Mountbatten gave a complete home cinema.

The Government of Canada sent a priceless collection of Georgian silver, and a mink coat, which now resides in the Palace refrigerator with a dozen others owing to the atmosphere of 'political correctness' about wearing fur.

West African troops were each ordered to give a penny towards a wedding present, while the Aga Khan gave a racehorse. The Girl Guides of Australia sent the ingredients for the wedding cake and Mahatma Gandhi gave a tray cloth he had woven himself.

When the presents went on display at St James's Palace, the proceeds went to charity. Princes Elizabeth's grandmother, Queen Mary, averted her eyes as she passed the tray cloth, thinking it was a loincloth and therefore unsuitable for a royal lady's eyes.

Diamonds, rubies, sapphires and pearls by the score were included in the official list; a set of crystal champagne glasses from Princess Margaret, Purdey guns for Philip…it went on and on.

Every one received an acknowledgement but not all found a home in a royal residence. Even today there are some, still in perfect condition, stored in an air-conditioned building in Windsor Home Park.

The total value of the royal couple's wedding presents amounted to a little over £2 million – and that was in 1947.

**Welsh Gold**

Since 1923, the wedding rings of every royal bride have been made from a single nugget of Welsh gold. It comes from a mine named Clogau St David's located at Bontddu (it means 'black bridge') in North Wales and was first presented to the late Queen Mother when, as Lady Elizabeth Bowes-Lyon, she married King George V's second son, Bertie, the Duke of York (later King George VI) at Westminster Abbey in 1923.

After the ring was made by W.J.L. Bertolle, Mr Bartholomew, the man who owned the mine, kept the rest of the gold nugget and refused to sell it to anyone else. In 1947, Princess Elizabeth was offered the gold for her wedding ring and, since then, Princess Margaret (1960), Princess Anne (1973), the Princess of Wales (1981), the Duchess of York (1986), the Countess of Wessex (1999) and the Duchess of Cornwall (2005) have each had their wedding rings made from the same gold, though, as only a tiny piece of the original was left in 1981, the Royal British Legion presented the Queen with a massive 36-gramme piece of 21-carat Welsh gold to supplement the stocks. This is held by the Crown Jewellers in readiness for any future royal weddings.

## Westminster Abbey

40 British Sovereigns have been crowned in Westminster Abbey with the first being William the Conqueror on Christmas Day 1066. Seventeen Monarchs are buried in the Abbey, together with 12 consorts and a number of their children.

Royal weddings at the Abbey are a comparatively modern tradition, with that of Princess Mary, the daughter of King George V, to Viscount Lascelles in 1922 being the first, followed closely the next year by the wedding of the Duke of York (later King George VI) to Lady Elizabeth Bowes-Lyon (later the Queen Mother).

Both the Queen (as Princess Elizabeth) in 1947 and her sister, Princess Margaret, in 1960, were married in Westminster Abbey, but the Prince of Wales was married to Lady Diana Spencer in St Paul's Cathedral in 1981, because it was felt more guests could be accommodated.

The Queen has her own stall in the Abbey and both clergy and lay officers are entitled to wear scarlet cassocks. It is also one of the few ecclesiastical buildings allowed to fly the Royal Standard because of its standing as a 'Royal Peculiar', an independent place of worship within the Church of England, not requiring allegiance to a diocese but responsible only to the Monarch who is the Abbey's Visitor.

The Order of the Bath has been associated with Westminster Abbey since its establishment in 1725 and the Order has adopted Henry VII's chapel for its own use. Both the banners of the Queen, Sovereign of the Order and the Prince of Wales, Great Master, hang at the west end of the chapel.

## Wine

Although the Palace cellars are stocked with hundreds of dozens of bottles of the finest vintage champagne, the Queen is believed not to care for it. At State Banquets when the toasts are being drunk, close observers have noticed that Her Majesty merely wets her lips, never taking even one swallow. Her favourite drink is gin and Dubonnet (⅔ gin to ⅓ Dubonnet) with ice added. But she does not like the sound of ice cubes grating against each other, so Prince Philip invented a machine that cleverly turns the ice cubes into tiny ice balls that rub gently together.

When the Royal couple are dining together in the evening they like to drink sweet German wine and Prince Philip also enjoys a glass or two of a beer called Double Diamond. It is brewed by Ind Coop and Alsop and, although it hasn't been on sale to the public for many years, it is still available to the brewery's most important single customer.

# X

❦

## X-Ray Machine at Buckingham Palace

The x-ray machine installed at Buckingham Palace is in fact a fluoroscope that is used by post offices and government departments throughout the world to detect anything suspicious that arrives by mail. The fluoroscope is widely used in medicine and also in industry to detect flaws in manufacture. Gamma rays, called phosphors, are directed at the object and they reveal anything that appears unnatural. Military installations have been using them for years.

Until recently, letters and parcels that were addressed to the Royal Family or members of the Royal Household were automatically delivered to the appropriate person or department without any inspection. But events in the last ten years have meant a complete overhaul of security arrangements at royal residences, as well as every other official building in the country.

Nothing is now left to chance and a small team of three, including the Flagman at the Palace, mans the machine through which mail is passed before it is considered safe to be delivered.

The fluoroscope was recommended by the Diplomatic and Royalty Protection Department, which guards not only the Royal Family but also every foreign Embassy and High Commission in London. They are not only looking for dangerous objects such as explosives and letter bombs, but anything unpleasant. Some people with a strange sense of humour try to send rotting food and other products, both animal and human, in an attempt to embarrass and humiliate those who live and work at the Palace. Nothing ever gets through. Unfortunately, the strict regulations mean that innocent packages are often also destroyed. At a time of celebration, boxes of chocolates, hand-made cakes and even gifts of clothing are sent, with every good intention. It makes little difference. Unless the Palace recognises the name of the donor, they are destroyed.

At one time, any unwanted gifts were distributed to worthy or charitable causes. Not any more. It would be too dangerous. Even baby clothes might have been treated with a substance that could cause harm or injury. That is why the x-ray machine is a vital piece of equipment in the Palace post office.

## Yachts

On 11 December 1997, Her Majesty's Royal Yacht *Britannia* was decommissioned in Portsmouth ending 43 years' service during which she sailed over one million nautical miles. It was the end of a chapter in British maritime history that began when Charles II, restored to the Monarchy in 1660, took possession of his first yacht, named the *Mary*, after his sister, the first Princess Royal. Since then, every Monarch has had a Royal Yacht, with *Britannia* being the 66th in a line that included three *Britannia*'s and three *Victoria and Albert*'s.

*Britannia* was the last ship in the Royal Navy in which the sailors (called Yotties) slept in hammocks, the only ship in the world who's captain was an admiral and the only ship that did not have her name displayed anywhere on her hull. The yacht was manned by 21 officers and 256 yachtsmen, plus a small Royal Marine Band of 26 musicians. The ship's company wore soft-soled shoes at all times, with all orders given by hand signal to preserve the tranquillity of a royal residence. When she was in port, no member of the crew was allowed ashore unless wearing a tie, and the yacht was also equipped with a garage for a Rolls-Royce.

During her lifetime, *Britannia* was used for four royal honeymoons:

Princess Margaret and the Earl of Snowdon (1960)
Princess Anne and Mark Phillips (1973)
The Prince and Princess of Wales (1981)

The Duke and Duchess of York (1986)
All four marriages failed, so Britannia's (below decks) nickname of 'The Love Boat' was not entirely appropriate, or appreciated by the Royal Family.

The Royal Yacht was launched by the Queen at Clydebank on Thursday, 16 April 1953, beginning a career that would see her travel a total of 1,087,623 nautical miles and carry out some 968 visits overseas and in home waters. The price paid for the yacht was £2,098,000 – undoubtedly the bargain of the century.

Since her decommissioning, *Britannia* has been found a permanent berth in Leith, Edinburgh, where she is open to the public all year round (subject to an entrance fee) and where there is also an exhibition and shop on the dockside.

## Yeomen of the Guard

There is often confusion between the Yeomen of the Guard and Yeomen Warders. Henry VII created the former in 1485 after the battle of Bosworth Field. They are the oldest of the royal bodyguards and the oldest military corps in the world. Originally chosen from the class of Yeomen or Gentlemen just below the rank of Esquire, they first appeared as escort to the Sovereign at the coronation of Henry VII and they have been in permanent attendance on the Sovereign ever since.

At the State Opening of Parliament, the Yeomen carry out the traditional searching of the vaults below the Houses of Parliament, since the 'Gunpowder Plot' of Guy Fawkes. They attend all royal ceremonial functions and can be seen at each Investiture, when they march into the State Ballroom at Buckingham Palace to the tune of 'Men of Harlech' (because they originally came from Wales) and at Royal Garden parties, they line the lane taken by the Queen as she progresses to the Royal tea marquee.

The headquarters of the Yeomen of the Guard is located in St James's Palace, where the members, who no longer are required to 'live in', keep their distinctive uniforms of scarlet doublet embroidered with a Tudor crown and the roses of York and Lancaster. These days their ranks are selected from retired, senior non-commissioned officers in the armed forces and they are not ordered to taste the royal food or sleep immediately outside the royal bedchamber, as they once did.

The Yeomen Warders are based at the Tower of London, where their duties include guarding the fortress. They are first mentioned in royal records during the reign of William the Conqueror when they guarded the White Tower and it was in 1549 that they helped Edward Seymour, Duke of Somerset, to escape from captivity.

On his release, he promised them anything they wanted and they replied that they wished to wear the same livery as the Yeomen of the Guard. The wish was granted and since then they have worn the same outfits with one difference: they do not wear the Guards' gold-embroidered cross-belt over the left shoulder. Both corps hate being taken for the other and it is the Yeomen Warders who are the 'Beefeaters', not the Yeomen of the Guard.

The full title of the Warders is: Yeomen Warders of Her Majesty's Royal Palace and Fortress the Tower of London, Members of the Yeomen of the Guard Extraordinary.

A new Yeomen Warder takes his oath of allegiance before the Resident Governor on Tower Green, once the Tower has closed for the evening. The oath dates back to 1337, when Edward III was on the throne. The new man is then toasted with the traditional words, 'May you never die a Yeomen Warder,' which may seem strange but they date back to the days when it was custom for Yeomen to sell their posts when they reached retirement age. That custom has long since ended but the practice of Yeomen Warders and their families living within the Tower of London continues. So they do enjoy living and working in one of the best addresses in the country and, as the Tower is one of the most popular tourist attractions in London, they are probably among the most photographed men (and now women, since they were admitted to the ranks in 2008) in the world.

There is a legend that if the ravens, who have inhabited the Tower since the reign of Charles II, ever leave, the kingdom will fall. Just to make sure this doesn't happen, the Yeoman Raven Master looks after the welfare of the remaining birds.

The term 'Beefeater' presumably refers to their diet of meat and, indeed, in 1813, the daily ration for 30 men on duty at St James's Palace was 24lb of beef, 18lb of mutton and 16lb of veal, so vegetarians need not apply.

## Y Bwthyn Bach

This is the Welsh name for the Little Cottage or Small House that was given by the people of Wales to the six-year-old Princess Elizabeth in 1932. It stands in the grounds of Royal Lodge (see Royal Lodge) in Windsor Great Park and, to all intents and purposes, it is a replica in miniature of a complete house with bedrooms, receptions rooms, kitchen and bathroom. The Princess, and later her sister, Princess Margaret, when she was older, loved to play in its tiny rooms, washing dishes and making the beds. Possibly the only time in either of their lives that they would perform such mundane household chores.

# Z

## Zara Phillips

The Queen's oldest granddaughter was born at 8.15pm on Friday, 15 May 1981 in the private Lindo Wing at St Mary's Hospital in Paddington, London. Four doctors assisted at the birth: the Royal Gynaecologist, George Pinker; the Queen's Physician, Sir Richard Baylis; Clive Roberts, Consultant Gynaecologist; and David Harvey, Anaesthetist. Zara weighed in at a healthy 8lb 1oz. Princess Anne chose the name Zara (a Greek biblical name meaning 'Bright as the Dawn') after Prince Charles suggested it.

The christening was a traditional royal ceremony, taking place in the Private Chapel at Windsor Castle at 11.45am on Monday, 27 July 1981, just two days before the wedding of the century with the Prince of Wales marrying Lady Diana Spencer.

There was a minor incident when Diana refused at the last minute to attend the service. The official reason given was that there were too many arrangements still left to finalise prior to her wedding. Unofficially, it was believed that Diana had heard that Camilla Parker Bowles was to be there with her then husband, Andrew Parker Bowles, one of the godfathers, and she did not want to socialise with the 'other' woman she suspected was still in her future husband's life.

At the christening, the Dean of Windsor, the Rt Rev Michael Mann, conducted the service, anointing the baby's head with holy water from the River Jordan, as she wore the robe of Honiton lace that has been worn by every royal baby since Queen Victoria's children were baptised.

The Queen and the Duke of Edinburgh were present with Prince Andrew being the senior godfather, along with the aforementioned Andrew Parker Bowles and Hugh Thomas, an

Olympic team-mate of Princess Anne's at the 1976 Games.

The godmothers were Helen (now Lady) Stewart, wife of the former World Champion racing driver, Sir Jackie Stewart, and the Countess of Lichfield, a long-time friend and Lady-in-Waiting to the Princess.

At the time of her birth, Zara was sixth in Line of Succession to the Throne; she is now twelfth, as her mother's siblings have produced children. She does not have a title, even an 'Honourable' to her name, on her mother's express wishes, and against those of the Queen.

But she has earned two major sporting titles: European Three-Day Event Champion in 2005, followed within 12 months by the World Championship in Aachen in Germany in August 2006. She then won the BBC Sports Personality of the Year in 2006.

She has proved she is among the best in the world at her sport and her popularity has increased interest in equestrianism immeasurably. The lack of an official royal title does not appear to have hindered her progress, but she does admit that her royal connections have opened certain doors.

# Appendix I

Appointments and Ranks Held By Members of the Royal
Family in Her Majesty's Armed Services,
and Commonwealth Armed Services
(Including Members of Foreign Royal Families)

## 1. HM THE QUEEN

A. ROYAL NAVY: Lord High Admiral of the United Kingdom [1964]

(1) Special Relationships:

    (a) HMS INVINCIBLE [3 May 1977]
    (b) HMS LANCASTER [24 May 1990]
    (c) HMS OCEAN [1997]

B. ARMY:

(1) Colonel-in-Chief:

    (a) The Life Guards [6 Feb 1952]
    (b) The Blues and Royals (Royal Horse Guards and 1st
        Dragoons) [1 Apr 1969]
    (c) The Royal Scots Dragoon Guards (Carabiniers and Greys)
        [2 Jul 1971]
    (d) The Queen's Royal Lancers [6 Jun 1993]
    (e) Royal Tank Regiment [2 Jun 1953]
    (f) Corps of Royal Engineers [6 Feb 1952]
    (g) Grenadier Guards [6 Feb 1952]
    (h) Coldstream Guards [6 Feb 1952]
    (i) Scots Guards [6 Feb 1952]
    (j) Irish Guards [6 Feb 1952]

(k)  Welsh Guards [6 Feb 1952]
(l)  The Royal Regiment of Scotland [28 Mar 2006]
(m) The Duke of Lancaster's Regiment (King's, Lancashire and Border) [1 Jul 2006]
(n)  The Royal Welsh [1 Mar 2006]
(o)  Adjutant General's Corps [6 Apr 1992]
(p)  The Royal Mercian and Lancastrian Yeomanry [1 Nov 1992]

*Ceasing:*
*The Queen's Lancashire Regiment [25 Mar 1970–1 Jul 2006]*
*The Argyll and Sutherland Highlanders (Princess Louise's)*
    *[22 Apr 1947–28 Mar 2006]*
*The Royal Green Jackets [1 Jan 1966–1 Feb 2007]*

(2)  Commonwealth Forces – Colonel-in-Chief:

(a)  The Governor General's Horse Guards [of Canada] [1988]
(b)  The King's Own Calgary Regiment (Royal Canadian Armoured Corps) [1953]
(c)  Canadian Military Engineers Branch [1977]
(d)  Royal 22e Regiment [of Canada] [1953]
(e)  Governor General's Foot Guards [of Canada] [1953]
(f)  The Canadian Grenadier Guards [1953]
(g)  Le Régiment de la Chaudière [of Canada] [1952]
(h)  2nd Battalion Royal New Brunswick Regiment (North Shore) [1953]
(i)  48th Highlanders of Canada [1952]
(j)  The Argyll and Sutherland Highlanders of Canada (Princess Louise's) [1952]
(k)  The Calgary Highlanders [1981]
(l)  Royal Australian Engineers
(m) Royal Australian Infantry Corps
(n)  Royal Australian Army Ordnance Corps
(o)  Royal Australian Army Nursing Corps
(p)  The Corps of Royal New Zealand Engineers
(q)  Royal New Zealand Infantry Regiment
(r)  The Malawi Rifles
(s)  The Royal Malta Artillery

(3)  Affiliated Colonel-in-Chief:

    (a)  The Queen's Gurkha Engineers [7 Sep 1993]

(4)  Captain General:

    (a)  Royal Regiment of Artillery [6 Feb 1952]
    (b)  The Honourable Artillery Company [6 Feb 1952]
    (c)  Combined Cadet Force [2 Jun 1953]

(5)  Commonwealth Forces – Captain General:

    (a)  Royal Regiment of Canadian Artillery [1953]
    (b)  Royal Regiment of Australian Artillery
    (c)  Royal Regiment of New Zealand Artillery
    (d)  Royal New Zealand Armoured Corps

(6)  Royal Colonel:

    (a)  The Argyll and Sutherland Highlanders, 5th Battalion
        The Royal Regiment of Scotland [28 Mar 2006]

(7)  Patron:

    (a)  Royal Army Chaplains' Department [6 Feb 1992]

C.  ROYAL AIR FORCE:

(1)  Air Commodore-in-Chief:

    (a)  Royal Auxiliary Air Force [1 Jun 1953]
    (b)  Royal Air Force Regiment [1 Jun 1953]

(2)  Commonwealth Forces – Air Commodore-in-Chief:

    (a)  Air Reserve of Canada [1953]
    (b)  Royal Australian Air Force Reserve
    (c)  Territorial Air Force (of New Zealand)

(3)  Commandant-in-Chief:

    (a)  Royal Air Force College Cranwell [27 May 1960]

(4)  Royal Honorary Air Commodore:

    (a)  Royal Air Force Marham [11 Jun 1977]
    (b)  603 (City of Edinburgh) Squadron Royal Auxiliary Air
        Force [1 Dec 2000]

## 2. HRH THE DUKE OF EDINBURGH

A. ROYAL NAVY:

(1) Rank:

    (a) Admiral of the Fleet [15 Jan 1953]

(2) Commonwealth Forces - Ranks:

    (a) Admiral of the Fleet Royal Australian Navy  [1 Apr 1954]
    (b) Admiral of the Fleet Royal New Zealand Navy [15 Jan 1953]
    (c) Admiral of the Royal Canadian Sea Cadets [15 Jan 1953]

B. ROYAL MARINES: Captain General Royal Marines [1 Jun 1953]

C. ARMY:

(1) Rank:

    (a) Field Marshal [15 Jan 1953]

(2) Commonwealth Forces - Ranks:

    (a) Field Marshal Australian Military Forces [1 Apr 1954]
    (b) Field Marshal New Zealand Army [11 Jun 1977]

(3) Colonel-in-Chief:

    (a) The Queen's Royal Hussars (Queen's Own and Royal Irish) [10 Apr 2002]
    (b) The Rifles [1 Feb 2007]
    (c) Corps of Royal Electrical and Mechanical Engineers [1 Jul 1969]
    (d) Intelligence Corps [11 Jun 1977]
    (e) Army Cadet Force Association [15 Jan 1953]

*Ceasing:*
*The Highlanders ( Seaforth,Gordons and Camerons)*
    *[17 Sep 1994–28 Mar 2006]*
*The Royal Gloucestershire, Berkshire and Wiltshire Regiment*
    *[27 Apr 1994–1 Feb 2007]*

(4) Commonwealth Forces – Colonel-in-Chief:

    (a) The Royal Canadian Regiment [1953]
    (b) The Royal Hamilton Light Infantry (Wentworth Regiment of Canada) [1978]

(c) The Cameron Highlanders of Ottawa [1967]
(d) The Queen's Own Cameron Highlanders of Canada [1967]
(e) The Seaforth Highlanders of Canada [1967]
(f) The Royal Canadian Army Cadets [1953]
(g) The Royal Australian Corps of Electrical and Mechanical Engineers [1959]
(h) The Australian Army Cadet Corps [1963]

(5) Colonel:

(a) Grenadier Guards [1 Mar 1975]

(6) Royal Colonel:

(a) The Highlanders. 4th Battalion, The Royal Regiment of Scotland [28 Mar 2006]

(7) Royal Honorary Colonel:

(a) City of Edinburgh Universities Officers Training Corps [23 Mar 1994]

(8) Commonwealth Forces – Royal Honorary Colonel:

(a) The Trinidad and Tobago Regiment [1964]

(9) Member:

(a) Honourable Artillery Company [1957]

## D. ROYAL AIR FORCE:

(1) Ranks:

(a) Marshal of the Royal Air Force [15 Jan 1953]

(2) Commonwealth Forces – Ranks:

(a) Marshal of the Royal Australian Air Force [1 Apr 1954]
(a) Marshal of the Royal New Zealand Air Force [11 Jun 1977]

(3) Air Commodore-in-Chief:

(a) Air Training Corps [15 Jan 1953]
(a) Royal Canadian Air Cadets [1953]

(4) Royal Honorary Air Commodore:

(a) Royal Air Force Kinloss [11 Jun 1977]

## 3. HRH THE PRINCE OF WALES

### A. ROYAL NAVY:

(1) Ranks

    (a) Admiral [14 Nov 2006]

(2) Commodore-in-Chief:

    (a) Plymouth [Aug 2006]

### B. ARMY:

(1) Rank:

    (a) General [14 Nov 2006]

(2) Colonel-in-Chief:

    (a) 1st The Queen's Dragoon Guards [1 Jul 2003]
    (b) The Royal Dragoon Guards [31 Jul 1992]
    (c) The Mercian Regiment [1 Sep 2007]
    (d) The Parachute Regiment [11 Jun 1977]
    (e) The Royal Gurkha Rifles [1 Jul 1994]
    (f) Army Air Corps [6 Feb 1992]

*Ceasing:*
*The King's Regiment [1 Jul 2003–1 Jul 2006]*
*The Cheshire (22nd) Regiment [11 Jun 1977–1 Sep 2007]*
*The Royal Regiment of Wales (24th/41st Foot)*
    *[1 Jul 1969–1 Mar 2006]*
*The Black Watch [28 Mar 2006]*

(3) Commonwealth Forces – Colonel-in-Chief:

    (a) The Royal Canadian Dragoons [1985]
    (b) Lord Strathcona's Horse (Royal Canadians) [1977]
    (c) Royal Regiment of Canada (10th Royal Grenadiers) [1977]
    (d) Royal Winnipeg Rifles [1977]
    (e) The Black Watch (Royal Highland Regiment) of Canada [Feb 2004]
    (f) The Toronto Scottish Regiment [Jan 2005]
    (g) Royal Australian Armoured Corps
    (h) The Royal Pacific Islands Regiment

(4) Colonel:

    (a) Welsh Guards [1 Mar 1975]

(5) Royal Colonel:

    (a) The Black Watch, 3rd Battalion The Royal Regiment of Scotland [28 Mar 2006]

    (b) 51st Highland, 7th Battalion The Royal Regiment of Scotland [28 Mar 2006]

(6) Royal Honorary Colonel:

    (a) The Queen's Own Yeomanry [17 Jun 2000]

(7) Member:

    (a) Honourable Artillery Company [1970]

C. ROYAL AIR FORCE:

(1) Rank:

    (a) Air Chief Marshal [14 Nov 2006]

(2) Royal Honorary Air Commodore:

    (a) Royal Air Force Valley [1 Apr 1993]

(3) Commonwealth Forces – Air Commodore-in-Chief:

    (a) Royal New Zealand Air Force [11 Jun 1977]

(4) Commonwealth Forces – Colonel in Chief:

    (a) Air Reserve [of Canada] [1977]

## 4. HRH PRINCE WILLIAM OF WALES

A. ROYAL NAVY:

(1) Rank:

    (a) Lieutenant [1 Jan 2009]

(2) Commodore-in-Chief:

    (a) Scotland [Aug 2006]

    (b) Submarines [Aug 2006]

B. ARMY:

(1) Rank:

    (a) Captain [1 Jan 2009]

C. ROYAL AIR FORCE:

(1) Rank:

    (a) Flight Lieutenant [1 Jan 2009]

(2) Royal Honorary Air Commandant:

    (a) Royal Air Force Coningsby [10 Sep 2008]

## 5. HRH PRINCE HENRY OF WALES

A. ROYAL NAVY:

(1) Commodore-in-Chief:

    (a) Small ships and diving [Aug 2006]

B. ARMY:

(1) Rank:

    (a) Lieutenant [Dec 2007]

    C. ROYAL AIR FORCE:

(1) Royal Honorary Air Commandant:

    (a) Royal Air Force Honington [10 Sep 2008]

## 6. HRH THE DUKE OF YORK

A. ROYAL NAVY:

(1) Rank:

    (a) Captain [Jun 05] Rear-Admiral [Feb 2010]

(2) Commodore-in-Chief:

    (a) Fleet Air Arm [Aug 2006]

B. SEA CADET CORPS:

(1) Admiral of the Sea Cadet Corps [11 May 1992]

C. ARMY:

(1) Colonel-in-Chief:

    (a) 9th/12th Royal Lancers (Prince of Wales's) [1 Jul 2003]
    (b) The Yorkshire Regiment (14th/15th, , 19th and 33rd/76th Foot)[6 Jun 2006]
    (c) The Royal Irish Regiment (27th (Inniskilling), 83rd, 87th and The Ulster Defence
    (d) Regiment) [1 Jun 1992]
    (e) Small Arms School Corps [1 Jul 2003]

*Ceasing:*
*The Royal Highland Fusiliers (Princess Margaret's Own Glasgow and Ayrshire*
*Regiment) [1 Jul 2003–28 Mar 2006]*
*The Staffordshire Regiment (The Prince of Wales's)*
*[21 Apr 1989–1 Sep 2007]*

(2) Commonwealth Forces – Colonel-in-Chief:

    (a) The Queen's York Rangers (First Americans) [1997]
    (b) Royal Highland Fusiliers of Canada [2005]
    (c) Princess Louise Fusiliers (Canada) [2005]
    (d) Royal New Zealand Army Logistics Regiment

(3) Royal Colonel:

    (a) The Royal Highland Fusiliers, 2nd Battalion The Royal Regiment of Scotland [28 Mar 2006]

(4) Member:

    (a) Honourable Artillery Company [1987]

D. ROYAL AIR FORCE:

(1) Royal Honorary Air Commodore:

    (a) Royal Air Force Lossiemouth [15 Sep 1996]

## 7. HRH THE EARL OF WESSEX

A. ROYAL NAVY:

(1) Commodore-in-Chief:
    (a) Royal Fleet Auxiliary [Aug 2006]

**B. ARMY:**

(1)  Royal Colonel:

    (a)  2nd Battalion The Rifles [1 Feb 2007]

(2)  Royal Honorary Colonel:

    (a)  The Royal Wessex Yeomanry [1 Jul 2003]

(3)  Commonwealth Forces – Colonel-in-Chief:

    (a)  The Hastings and Prince Edward Regiment [18 Oct 2002]
    (b)  Saskatchewan Dragoons [Jun 2003]
    (c)  Prince Edward Island Regiment [Dec 2004]

**C. ROYAL AIR FORCE:**

(1)  Royal Honorary Air Commodore:

    (a)  Royal Air Force Waddington [10 Sep 2008]

## 8. HRH THE PRINCESS ROYAL

**A. ROYAL NAVY:**

(1)  Vice Admiral Chief Commandant for Women in the Royal
Navy [1 Dec 2009]
*(Previously Chief Commandant, Women's Royal Naval Service
[1 Jul 1974])*

(2)  Special Relationships:

    (a)  HMS TALENT [15 Apr 1988]
    (b)  HMS ALBION [9 Mar 2001]

(3)  Commodore-in-Chief:

    (a)  Portsmouth [Aug 2006]

**B. ARMY:**

(1)  Colonel-in-Chief:

    (a)  The King's Royal Hussars [4 Dec 1992]
    (b)  Royal Corps of Signals [11 Jun 1977]
    (c)  Royal Logistic Corps [5 Apr 1993]
    (d)  Royal Army Veterinary Corps [1 Jul 2003]

*Ceasing:*

*The Royal Scots (The Royal Regiment) [30 Jun 1983–1 Aug 2006]*
*The Worcestershire and Sherwood Foresters Regiment (29th/45th Foot)*
*[28 Feb 1970–1 Sep 2007]*

(2)   Commonwealth Forces – Colonel-in-Chief:

- (a)   8th Canadian Hussars (Princess Louise's) [1972]
- (b)   Royal Newfoundland Regiment [1988]
- (c)   Canadian Forces Communications and Electronics Branch [1977]
- (d)   The Grey and Simcoe Foresters [Royal Canadian Armoured Corps] [1977]
- (e)   The Royal Regina Rifle Regiment [1982]
- (f)   Canadian Forces Medical Services [2003]
- (g)   Royal Australian Corps of Signals
- (h)   Royal New Zealand Corps of Signals
- (i)   Royal New Zealand Nursing Corps

(3)   Affiliated Colonel-in-Chief:

- (a)   The Queen's Gurkha Signals [7 Sep 1993]
- (b)   The Queen's Own Gurkha Transport Regiment [7 Sep 1993]

(4)   Colonel:

- (a)   The Blues and Royals (Royal Horse Guards and 1st Dragoons) [1 Sep 1998]

(5)   Royal Colonel:

- (a)   The Royal Scots Borderers, 1st Battalion The Royal Regiment of Scotland [28 Mar 2006]
- (b)   52nd Lowland, 6th Battalion The Royal Regiment of Scotland [28 Mar 2006]

(6)   Royal Honorary Colonel:

- (a)   University of London Officers Training Corps [21 Apr 1989]

(7)   Commandant in Chief:

- (a)   First Aid Nursing Yeomanry (Princess Royals Volunteer Corps) [1981]

(8)   Member:

    (a)   Honourable Artillery Company [2004]

## C.  ROYAL AIR FORCE:

(1)   Royal Honorary Air Commodore:

    (a)   Royal Air Force Lyneham [11 Jun 1977]
    (b)   University of London Air Squadron [2 Sep 1993]

## 9.  HRH THE DUCHESS OF CORNWALL

### A.  ROYAL NAVY:

(1)   Special Relationship:

    (a)   HMS ASTUTE

(2)   Commodore-in-Chief:

    (a)   Naval Medical Services [Aug 2006]
    (b)   Naval Chaplaincy Services [2 Oct 2008]

### B.  ARMY:

(1)   Colonel-in-Chief:

    (a)   Special Reconnaissance Regiment [23 Aug 2008]

(2)   Royal Colonel:

    (a)   4th Battalion The Rifles [1 Feb 2007]

### C.  ROYAL AIR FORCE:

(1)   Royal Honorary Air Commodore:

    (a)   Royal Air Force Halton [10 Sep 2008]
    (b)   Royal Air Force Leeming [10 Sep 2008]

## 10.  HRH THE COUNTESS OF WESSEX

### A.  ROYAL NAVY:

(1)   Special Relationship:

    (a)   HMS DARING

B. ARMY:

(1)  Colonel-in-Chief:

   (a)  Queen Alexandra's Royal Army Nursing Corps [1 Jul 2003]
   (b)  Corps of Army Music [1 Sep 2007]

(2)  Royal Colonel:

   (a)  5th Battalion The Rifles [1 Feb 2007]

(3)  Commonwealth Forces – Colonel-in-Chief:

   (a)  Lincoln and Welland Regiment [Oct 2004]
   (b)  South Alberta Light Horse [Apr 2006]

C. ROYAL AIR FORCE:

(1)  Royal Honorary Air Commodore:

   (a)  Royal Air Force Wittering [10 Sep 2008]

## 11.  HRH THE DUKE OF GLOUCESTER

A. ARMY:

(1)  Colonel-in-Chief:

   (a)  The Royal Anglian Regiment [21 Apr 2006]
   (b)  Royal Army Medical Corps [1 Jul 2003]

(2)  Commonwealth Forces – Colonel-in-Chief:

   (a)  Royal New Zealand Army Medical Corps [2008]

(3)  Deputy Colonel-in-Chief:

   (a)  The Royal Logistic Corps [5 Apr 1993]

   *Ceasing:*
   *The Royal Gloucestershire, Berkshire and Wiltshire Regiment*
   *[27 Apr 1994–1 Feb 2007]*

(4)  Royal Colonel:

   (a)  6th Battalion, The Rifles [1 Feb 2007]

(5)  Royal Honorary Colonel:

   (a)  Royal Monmouthshire Royal Engineers (Militia)
       [11 Jun 1977]

B. ROYAL AIR FORCE:

(1) Rank:

    (a) Honorary Air Marshal [1 Sep 1996]

(2) Royal Honorary Air Commodore:

    (a) Royal Air Force Odiham [1 Apr 1993]
    (b) No 501 (County of Gloucester) Squadron Royal Auxiliary Air Force [5 Jun 2001]

## 12. HRH THE DUCHESS OF GLOUCESTER

A. ROYAL NAVY:

(1) Special Relationship:

    (a) HMS GLOUCESTER [2 Nov 1982]

B. ARMY:

(1) Colonel-in-Chief:

    (a) Royal Army Dental Corps [17 Jun 2000]

(2) Commonwealth Forces – Colonel-in-Chief:

    (a) Canadian Forces Dental Services [2006]
    (b) Royal Australian Army Educational Corps
    (c) Royal New Zealand Army Educational Corps

(3) Colonial Forces – Colonel-in-Chief:

    (a) The Bermuda Regiment [6 Nov 2003]

(4) Deputy Colonel-in-Chief:

    (a) Adjutant General's Corps [6 Apr 1992]

(5) Royal Colonel:

    (a) 7th Battalion, The Rifles [1 Feb 2007]

## 13. HRH THE DUKE OF KENT

A. ARMY:

(1) Rank:

    (a) Field Marshal [11 Jun 1993]

(2) Colonel-in-Chief:

    (a) The Royal Regiment of Fusiliers [1 Jul 1969]

    *Ceasing:*
    *The Devonshire and Dorset Regiment [11 Jun 1977–1 Feb 2007]*

(3) Commonwealth Forces – Colonel-in-Chief:

    (a) The Lorne Scots (Peel, Dufferin and Halton Regiment) [1977]

(4) Deputy Colonel-in-Chief:

    (a) The Royal Scots Dragoon Guards (Carabiniers and Greys) [2 Dec 1993]

(5) Colonel:

    (a) Scots Guards [9 Sep 1974]

(6) Royal Colonel:

    (a) 1st Battalion The Rifles [1 Feb 2007]

(7) Member:

    (a) Honourable Artillery Company [1967]

B. ROYAL AIR FORCE:

(1) Rank:

    (a) Honorary Air Chief Marshal [1 Jul 1996]

(2) Royal Honorary Air Commodore:

    (a) Royal Air Force Leuchars [1 Apr 1993]

## 14. HRH THE DUCHESS OF KENT

A. ARMY:

(1) Rank:

    (a) Honorary Major General [28 Feb 1967]

(2) Deputy Colonel-in-Chief:

    (a) The Royal Dragoon Guards [31 Jul 1992]

    (b)  The Royal Logistic Corps [5 Apr 1993]
    (c)  Adjutant General's Corps [6 Apr 1992]

## 15.  HRH PRINCE MICHAEL OF KENT

A.  ROYAL NAVY:

(1)  Rank:

    (a)  Honorary Rear Admiral Royal Naval Reserve [1 Jun 2004]

(2)  Commodore-in-Chief :

    (a)  Maritime Reserves [Aug 2006]

B.  ARMY:

(1)  Rank:

    (a)  Major (Retired) The Royal Hussars (Prince of Wales's Own)

(2)  Honorary Colonel

    (a)  Honourable Artillery Company [Jul 2009]

(3)  Commonwealth Forces – Colonel-in-Chief:

    (a)  Essex and Kent Scottish Regiment, Ontario [2004]

C.  ROYAL AIR FORCE:

(1)  Royal Honorary Air Commodore:

    (a)  Royal Air Force Benson [27 Jun 2002]

## 16.  HRH PRINCESS MICHAEL OF KENT

A.  ROYAL  NAVY:

(1)  Special Relationship:

    (a)  HMS PENZANCE [11 Mar 1997]

## 17.  HRH PRINCESS ALEXANDRA, THE HON LADY OGILVY

A.  ROYAL NAVY:

(1)  Special Relationship:

    (a)  HMS KENT [27 May 1998]

(2) Patron:

    (a) Queen Alexandra's Royal Naval Nursing Service
    [12 Nov 1955]

## B. ARMY:

(1) Royal Colonel:

    (a) 3rd Battalion The Rifles [1 Feb 2007]

*Ceasing: Colonel in Chief The King's Own Royal Border Regiment
[11 Jun 1977– 01 Jul 2006]
The Light Infantry [10 Apr 2002–1 Feb 2007]*

(2) Commonwealth Forces – Royal Colonel:

    (a) The Queen's Own Rifles of Canada [1960]
    (b) The Canadian Scottish Regiment (Princess Mary's) [1977]

(3) Deputy Colonel-in-Chief:

    (a) The Queen's Royal Lancers [25 Jun 1993]

(4) Royal Honorary Colonel:

    (a) The Royal Yeomanry [10 Apr 2002]

## C. ROYAL AIR FORCE:

(1) Patron and Air Chief Commandant:

    (a) Princess Mary's Royal Air Force Nursing Service [1 Nov 1966]

(2) Royal Honorary Air Commodore:

    (a) Royal Air Force Cottesmore [15 Sep 2000]

## 18. HONORARY RANKS AND APPOINTMENTS HELD BY FOREIGN ROYALTY

### A. ROYAL NAVY:

(1) HM The King of Sweden KG – Admiral [25 Jun 1975]

(2) HM The Sultan of Brunei GCB GCMG – Admiral [4 Aug 2001]

### B. ROYAL MARINES:

(1) HM King Harald V of Norway KG GCVO – Colonel [1981]

## C. ARMY:

(1) HM The Sultan of Brunei GCB GCMG – General [23 Feb 1984]

(2) HM King Harald V of Norway KG GCVO – General [5 Jul 1994]

*Ceasing:*
*Colonel-in-Chief The Green Howards (Alexandra, Princess of*
*    Wales's Own*
*Yorkshire Regiment) [6 Feb 1992–6 Jun 2006]*

(3) HRH The Grand Duke Jean of Luxembourg KG – General
[17 Mar 1995]

(4) HRH The Grand Duke of Luxembourg GCVO – Major The
Parachute Regiment [19 Jul 1989]

(5) HRH Prince Mohamed Bolkiah of Brunei CVO – Lieutenant
Irish Guards [15 Nov 1971]

(6) HM Queen Margrethe II of Denmark KG – Colonel-in-Chief
The Princess of Wales's Royal Regiment (Queen's and Royal
Hampshires) [25 Feb 1997]

(7) HM King Abdullah of Jordan KCVO – Colonel-in-Chief The
Light Dragoons [1 Jul 2003] [2nd Lt 11 Apr 1981]

## D. ROYAL AIR FORCE:

(1) HM The Sultan of Brunei GCB GCMG – Air Chief Marshal
[1992]

# Appendix II

## The Honours System

Most honours are announced nowadays in one of the two sets of honours lists – one at the New Year and the other in June on the occasion of the Sovereigns Official Birthday. Though, as Her Majesty is the fount of all honours, she may award decorations at other times at her discretion.

There are nine orders in the British honours system. These are:

The Order of the Garter* (1 class)
The Order of the Thistle** (1 class)
The Order of the Bath (3 classes)
The Order of St Michael and St George (3 classes)
The Royal Victorian Order (5 classes)
The Order of Merit (1 class)
The Royal Victorian Chain (1 class)
The Order of the British Empire (5 classes)
Order of the Companions of Honour (1 class)

* In the case of the Orders of the Garter and Thistle, new knights are appointed when a vacancy occurs and on their respective patron saint days.

The order of St John is the tenth Order. Unlike the Orders above it is not a State Order and recommendations for membership are submitted by the Grand Prior to the Queen who is Sovereign Head.

## ** Knights Bachelor

A knight may be either Knights Bachelor or a member of one of the Orders of Chivalry. In the former case this dignity had its origin in Britain from Saxon times. The majority of newly appointed knights are made Knights Bachelor.

## Gallantry Awards

There are eight main gallantry awards awarded under the British Honours system. These are subdivided into three levels of gallantry. A further three awards can be given for gallantry or distinguished services.

### Level 1

#### I) Victoria Cross – instituted in 1856.

For most conspicuous bravery or some daring or pre-eminent act of valour or self sacrifice or extreme devotion to duty in the presence of the enemy.

#### II) George Cross – instituted in 1940.

It may be awarded for acts of the greatest heroism or of the most conspicuous courage in circumstances of extreme danger. The cross is intended primarily for civilians. Awards within the armed services are confined to actions for which purely military honours are not normally granted. It is awarded for actions not in the face of the enemy.

### Level 2

#### I) Conspicuous Gallantry Cross – instituted in 1995.

Awarded to all ranks of all three services for conspicuous gallantry and great heroism.

#### II) George Medal – instituted in 1940.

Awarded only for acts of great bravery and it is intended primarily for civilians. Award to the military services is confined to actions for which purely military honours are not normally granted.

### III) Distinguished Service Order

Established in 1886 for rewarding individual instances of meritorious distinguished service in war or during an armed conflict.

## Level 3

### I) Military Cross – first instituted in 1914.

Awarded to all ranks of all three services for gallant and distinguished services in action on land.

### II) Distinguished Service Cross – first award dates from 1914 (having been first instituted, as the conspicuous Service Cross in 1901).

Awarded to all ranks of all three services for gallant and distinguished services in action at sea.

### III) Distinguished Flying Cross – first instituted in 1918.

Awarded to all ranks of all three services for gallant and distinguished services in action in the air.

### IV) Queen's Gallantry Medal – first instituted in 1974.

Recognises acts of exemplary bravery and intended primarily for civilians but may be awarded to military personnel engaged in a civilian scenario.

### V) Royal Red Cross Class I – first instituted in 1883.

Awarded to fully trained nurses of the Armed Services for acts of bravery and devotion to duty.

### VI) Air Force Cross – first instituted in 1918.

Awarded to all ranks of all three services for acts of valour, courage or devotion to duty whilst in the air but not in the face of the enemy.

### Order Collars

The Orders of the Garter and the Thistle, together with the 1st class of the Orders of the Bath, St Michael and St George, Royal Victoria Orders and British Empire entitle the holder to wear a Collar chain. The Collar is worn on prescribed Collar days e.g.

the Queen's Birthday, Patron Saint days, State Opening of Parliament etc. The Collar and Broad riband or sash are not worn simultaneously.

All collars are returnable on the death of the Knight or Dame

### Foreign Orders and Decorations

Most members of the Royal Family have, through the course of their lives, been awarded various Foreign Orders and Decorations. These are either as a result of incoming State Visits to the UK or through their official visits abroad.

The Star and broad riband or sash are generally only worn in the country concerned or in the presence of the head of state who originally awarded it. The miniatures of the award, worn on a miniature medal bar, can be seen more frequently at State Banquets. The annual Diplomatic reception or at Buckingham Palace and at formal evening events abroad.

# Appendix III

## Medals and Decorations Worn by Members of the Royal Family

### The Queen

Imperial Order of the Crown of India
Defence medal
War medal 1939–45
King George V Silver Jubilee 1935
King George VI Coronation 1937
Canadian Forces Decoration

### The Duke of Edinburgh

Queen's Service Order, New Zealand
39–45 Star
Atlantic Star
Africa Star
Burma Star (Pacific)
Italy Star
War Medal 39–45 (MID)
Coronation 1937
Coronation 1953
Jubilee Medal 1977
Golden Jubilee 2002
New Zealand Commemoration 1990
Malta George Cross 50th Anniversary 1992
Greek War Cross 1950
France Croix de Guerre Palm 39–45

## Prince of Wales

Queen's Service Order (New Zealand)
Queen Elizabeth II Coronation
Queen Elizabeth II Silver Jubilee
Queen Elizabeth II Golden Jubilee
Canadian Forces Decoration
New Zealand 1990 Commemoration medal

## Prince William

Queen Elizabeth II Golden Jubilee

## Prince Henry

Operational Service medal – Afghanistan
Queen Elizabeth II Golden Jubilee

## The Duke of York

South Atlantic medal
Queen Elizabeth II Silver Jubilee
Queen Elizabeth II Golden Jubilee
Canadian Forces Decoration
New Zealand 1990 Commemoration medal

## The Earl of Wessex

Queen Elizabeth II Silver Jubilee
Queen Elizabeth II Golden Jubilee
New Zealand 1990 Commemoration medal

## The Princess Royal

Queen's Service Order (New Zealand)
Queen Elizabeth II Coronation
Queen Elizabeth II Silver Jubilee
Queen Elizabeth II Golden Jubilee
Canadian Forces Decoration
New Zealand 1990 Commemoration medal

# Select Bibliography

*Royal Encyclopedia*, Ed. Ronald Allison & Sarah Riddell, Macmillan 1991
*The Royal Handbook*, Alan Hamilton, Mitchell Beazley 1985
*Monarchy and the Royal Family*, Graham and Heather Fisher, Robert Hale 1979
*At Home with the Queen*, Brian Hoey, Harper Collins 2003
*Her Majesty*, Brian Hoey, Harper Collins 2001
*The Queen*, Ronald Allison, Harper Collins 2001
*Inside Buckingham Palace*, Andrew Morton, Michael O'Mara Books 1991
*Britannia*, Brian Hoey, Patrick Stephens Ltd 1995
*The Royal Train*, Brian Hoey, Haynes Publishing 2008